BERTIL ALBREKTSON

History and the Gods

An Essay on the Idea of Historical Events
as Divine Manifestations
in the Ancient Near East and in Israel

CWK GLEERUP LUND SWEDEN

The cost of printing has been subsidized by
Statens Humanistiska Forskningsråd

CONIVGI DILECTISSIMAE

Preface

The concluding lines of my previous work, *Studies in the Text and Theology of the Book of Lamentations*, stressed the contrast between the general Near Eastern belief in gods enthroned in inviolable temples and the Israelite faith in a Lord 'who reigns supreme in history'. The emphasis on Yhwh's rule in history as a distinctive feature of Hebrew religion echoed, of course, an opinion which has dominated Old Testament theology during the last decades. But the Mesha Stone and other extra-biblical texts subsequently made me wonder whether the current view was not in need of revision, and I began to study parallels to the Israelite idea of a divine rule and a divine revelation in historical events in the literature of the neighbouring peoples.

The results of that study are put forward in the present essay. I am fully aware that much remains to be said and that many important points have been treated rather briefly. This is partly due to circumstances beyond my control: the work is submitted in connexion with my application for a vacant chair in this University and therefore had to be printed before a certain date. The fact that the book had thus to be finished in a comparatively short time has left its inevitable traces. On the other hand I think I have said—however briefly—what I wanted to say and what I believe needs saying, and the comparative material should be full enough to establish my main points. It is hoped that the study will not be entirely without value as a contribution to the important question of the distinctiveness of Hebrew religion. Much of what is maintained in the essay is admittedly rather obvious, but as it is not always so regarded, it may still be worth saying. If many of my conclusions appear in the main negative, this is not at all because I want to deny that the Old Testament faith is something *sui generis* in the ancient Near East but because I believe it to be necessary to clear away false and all too facile definitions of its distinctiveness before we can hope to describe it correctly.

All Semitic texts are quoted in the original and in English translation. Though I have of course profited from existing translations, particularly where they have been available in English, the renderings are in principle my own; they are fairly literal and make no pretence to any literary qualities. The Akkadian texts had to be quoted from editions with somewhat differing systems of transcription, but I have attempted to make the transliterations reasonably consistent and in accordance with modern usage. The inconsistencies which still remain should not, I trust, cause any serious inconveniences. The fact that many of the Akkadian texts are accessible only in antiquated editions constitutes a considerable difficulty to one who, like myself, is an amateur in Assyriology, especially as von Soden's *Handwörterbuch* and the *Chicago Assyrian Dictionary* are still incomplete. It has therefore been of the utmost value to me to be able to draw on the expert advice of Professor J. Aro of the University of Helsinki on problems of transliteration and translation of passages in Akkadian. He made a number of helpful suggestions and criticisms to the original typescript and saved me from many errors. I am greatly indebted to him for his kind and unselfish help, which also included proof-reading. It goes without saying that the mistakes which remain are entirely my own.

In matters of chronology I have generally followed J. A. Brinkman's appendix on 'Mesopotamian Chronology of the Historical Period' in A. L. Oppenheim's *Ancient Mesopotamia,* Chicago and London 1964, pp. 335 ff.

Mr. F. R. Southerington, B. A., B. Litt. (Oxon.), Lecturer in English in Åbo Academy, kindly took the trouble to correct the English of my typescript; I thank him for his care.

A most generous grant from *Oscar och Signe Krooks Stiftelse,* administered by the Faculty of Theology in the University of Lund, enabled me to begin work on this study. I must also mention with gratitude a grant from Åbo Academy which made possible a study visit to the library of the Department of Oriental Studies in the University of Helsinki.

Finally I owe my wife a great debt of gratitude for her help in countless ways, not least in typing the whole manuscript.

B.A.

Åbo Academy
February 1967

8

Contents

Introduction

It has become a commonplace that 'history is the chief medium of revelation'[1] in the Old Testament. This assertion is not restricted to some particular school of thought or to the domain of a certain language: almost any standard work on Old Testament religion or theology written in the last decades will agree, more or less explicitly, that the 'knowledge of God was an inference from what actually had happened in human history'[2] and that 'Yhwh is the God of history and history is his foremost means of revelation'.[3]

When history is thus stressed as the medium of God's revelation in the Old Testament, this seems to be done in at least two different ways. As a rule emphasis is laid on history in contrast with some other medium of revelation. The first contrast is that between nature and history. It is often used to characterize the difference between ideas of revelation in the ancient Near East in general on one hand and the Old Testament view of revelation on the other. Mowinckel has given a very clear expression of this alleged contrast: 'While the other peoples experienced the deity in the eternal cyclic process of nature, the Israelites experienced God in history.'[4] Similar statements have been made by many leading Old Testament scholars of many different schools. M. Noth, in an article on the idea of history in Old Testament apocalyptic, has emphasized that the Old Testament tells so much about the history

---

[1] G. E. Wright, *God Who Acts. Biblical Theology as Recital* (SBT 8), London 1952, p. 13.

[2] Wright, op. cit., p. 44.

[3] E. Jacob, *La tradition historique en Israël* (Études théologiques et religieuses), Montpellier 1946, p. 12: 'Yahveh est le Dieu de l'histoire et l'histoire est son plus sûr moyen de révélation.'

[4] 'Medan de andra folken upplevde gudomen i naturens eviga kretslopp, upplevde israeliterna Gud i historien.' ('Den västorientaliska och israelitisk-judiska litteraturen', *Bonniers allmänna litteraturhistoria*, ed. E. N. Tigerstedt, I, Stockholm 1959, p. 40). Cf. the almost identical formulation by N. H. Ridderbos: 'Israëls „Umwelt" kent de goden uit de natuur; Israël kent zijn God uit de geschiedenis, verklaard door de profetie.' ('Het Oude Testament en de geschiedenis, II', *GThT* 58, 1958, p. 1; cf. also part I of the same article, *GThT* 57, 1957, pp. 113 f.).

of Israel and the neighbouring peoples precisely because this history was seen as a divine work, and he regards this as a point where Israel is fundamentally different from its environment: the religions of the ancient Near East traced the divine powers in the recurring interplay of the forces of nature, whereas the Old Testament finds God revealed in unrepeatable events of history.[5] The same contrast between revelation in nature and revelation in history is found also in Th. C. Vriezen's well-known work on the theology of the Old Testament: 'Israel did not derive its knowledge of God first and foremost from nature, as the ancient oriental peoples did, but from the acts of God in the history of the people . . .'.[6]

If history tends to be stressed in contrast to nature when the Israelite idea of revelation is compared with that of other peoples in the ancient Near East, it is also often emphasized in contrast to the word, especially in works of systematic theologians trying to define the typically biblical idea of revelation. The second pair of opposites, then, is word and history. The classical Christian view of the means of revelation, of course, laid stress upon the divine word in the Bible, but gradually this opinion has given way to a school of thought which emphasizes instead

---

[5] 'Denn offenbar nicht um ihrer selbst willen wird im Alten Testament so viel von der Geschichte Israels und auch von der Geschichte der Völker ringsum erzählt, sondern deswegen, weil innerhalb dieser Geschichte das Wirken Gottes erfahren wird. Gerade in dieser speziellen Hinsicht unterscheidet sich das Alte Testament fundamental von seiner Umgebung. Während es in den Religionen der altorientalischen Welt das ständig sich wiederholende Kräftespiel mythischer Mächte ist, in denen das übermenschliche Walten des Göttlichen angeschaut und verehrt wird, mag es sich um Himmel und Erde, um Gestirne und Elemente, um Leben und Tod handeln, wird im Alten Testament vorzugsweise geschichtlich Einmaliges als Kundgebung Gottes verstanden.' ('Das Geschichtsverständnis der alttestamentlichen Apokalyptik', *Arbeitsgemeinschaft für Forschung des Landes Nordrhein-Westfalen*, Geisteswissenschaften, H. 21, Köln und Opladen 1954, pp. 5 f. (=*Gesammelte Studien zum Alten Testament* (ThB 6), München 1957, p. 249).

[6] Th. C. Vriezen, *An Outline of Old Testament Theology*, Oxford 1958, p. 187. Vriezen emphasizes the importance of the idea of a revelation in history very strongly: 'One of the most characteristic elements of the Old Testament teaching concerning God is the great stress laid on *God's activity in history*. The belief in God seems to be wholly based on the experience of this activity. . . . Israel derives its knowledge of God from His activity in history on behalf of His people, particularly in Egypt and in the desert.' (p. 136; Vriezen's italics). In view of this marked emphasis on history as an almost exclusive means of divine revelation in the Old Testament it is somewhat surprising to find in the chapter on 'The revelation of God' (pp. 233–269) several sections on revelation through dreams, visions, the spirit, the word, the law, etc., but no section on 'history'. It is significant that this chapter is based on a detailed study of the texts—not so the sweeping claims for history as the supreme medium of revelation earlier in the book.

the action of God in history, his revelation in events.[7] This view is said to do more justice to the teaching of the biblical writings themselves, and especially the Old Testament is invoked in support of it. Again examples can easily be found in many theological works from the last decades. The point is pressed very hard in an article on revelation by G. S. Hendry: 'God reveals himself in his acts on the plane of history. The fundamental fact of OT faith is the liberation of Israel from the house of bondage . . .; it is by this act that God made himself known to Israel . . . For God acts in history, and through all that he does he makes himself known . . . God's mighty and gracious acts, however, often failed to achieve their revealing purpose because of the blindness and obtuseness of his people . . . So God raised up a special class of men to speak for him and to be interpreters of his work . . . These men, the prophets, became by an act of grace . . . the great agents of God's revelation of himself by his word. Yet the word is never to be thought of in an intellectualistic sense as the communication of abstract truth. The Heb. term for 'word' means also thing, act, event, and with God word and work are one . . .; the word of God is the speaking or significant side of his work.'[8] Here history is seen as the chief—indeed almost sole—medium of revelation: the divine word is only reluctantly accepted as a substitute, made necessary by Israel's regrettable inability to receive God's true revelation in the events of history. And even so the divine word is not allowed remain 'word' but somewhat forcibly subsumed into the all-important category of 'act'. In the beginning was the Deed; the word is an emergency measure. Hendry's view may seem rather extreme, but he is in fact only saying what a great many others have argued too, though perhaps not quite so frankly. After an examination of the idea of revelation in recent thought J. Baillie concludes: 'Our study has thus led us to the conclusion that revelation is always given us through events.'[9]

It is very difficult to decide whether it is this general tendency in recent theology to stress the idea of revelation through events that has inspired biblical scholars to emphasize history as a key-word in Old Testament theology, or whether exegetical studies have brought about this current view of revelation in biblical and systematic theology. It has probably been a two-way traffic. More important is the question of the basis for this modern tendency. To what extent can it be justified

---

[7] See e.g. J. Baillie, *The Idea of Revelation in Recent Thought*, New York 1956, esp. pp. 62 ff.

[8] G. S. Hendry, 'Reveal, Revelation', in *A Theological Word Book of the Bible*, ed. A. Richardson, London 1950, pp. 196 f.

[9] Op. cit., p. 78. Cf. also p. 132: '. . . all revelation is given through history'.

from the texts themselves? Too many slogans have been accepted and faithfully repeated from textbook to textbook with very scant foundations for such a question to be superfluous.

It goes without saying that a determination of what is peculiarly Israelite in this field could only be made on the basis of a detailed comparison with non-biblical texts. As a rule, however, the alleged contrast between the biblical and the general Near Eastern ideas of revelation is treated as something almost self-evident, which is not in need of further demonstration or proof. Often a sweeping statement seems to be regarded as sufficient, without references to the relevant texts or to the works of other scholars. This is all the more surprising as there are in fact a few scholars who have warned against too simple a contrasting of the Old Testament and the ancient Near Eastern views of history. J. Hempel[10] has pointed out that the idea of historical events as divine actions is not exclusively biblical but common to the whole Near East, and that even outside Israel misfortunes and disasters have been interpreted as divine judgments. Following Hempel, J. Lindblom has emphasized that 'The prophetic idea of Yahweh's activity in history was not quite unparalleled in the ancient world.'[11] These important reservations seem however not to have been much observed. Moreover, those who have uttered these warnings against too facile an antithesis between the Old Testament and other ancient documents on this particular point have done so rather briefly, without any detailed comparison between the relevant texts. Thus a more thorough investigation of the extra-biblical material seems justified.

The question of the relation between words and events in the Old Testament view of revelation has attracted more interest than the problem of the relation between Israelite and general Near Eastern ideas of history. As is well known, it is at present the subject of an interesting discussion in which both biblical scholars and systematic theologians are taking part. 'Revelation as history' is the motto of W. Pannenberg and his school,[12] and the Old Testament is an important

---

[10] *Altes Testament und Geschichte* (Studien des apologetischen Seminars 27), Gütersloh 1930, pp. 9 ff. Cf. also the same author's *Geschichten und Geschichte im Alten Testament bis zur persischen Zeit*, Gütersloh 1964, pp. 86 f.

[11] *Prophecy in Ancient Israel*, Oxford 1962, p. 324. See also A. Weiser, *Glaube und Geschichte im Alten Testament* (BWANT 4: 4), Stuttgart 1931, pp. 47 f. (=*Glaube und Geschichte im Alten Testament und andere ausgewählte Schriften*, Göttingen 1961, pp. 137 f.) (though with some criticisms of Hempel), and W. Eichrodt, *Theologie des Alten Testaments* I, Leipzig 1933, pp. 9 f.

[12] See above all the joint work edited by W. Pannenberg with contributions also by R. Rendtorff, U. Wilckens, and T. Rendtorff: *Offenbarung als Geschichte* (KuD Beiheft 1), Göttingen 1961, 3. Aufl. 1965.

armoury not only for their Old Testament specialist, R. Rendtorff, but also for Pannenberg himself, a systematic theologian. Their exegetical arguments have however not met with general acceptance, and Old Testament scholars such as W. Zimmerli[13] and F. Hesse[14] have raised important objections. At the same time—and independently of this discussion—J. Barr[15] has vigorously challenged the current belief that the formula 'revelation through history' faithfully represents the characteristic Old Testament review.

The main purpose of the present essay is to examine the more neglected question whether the Old Testament idea of historical events as divine manifestations is quite as distinctive as is commonly claimed. The Hebrew view itself is well-known and has often been investigated, and no one denies that it is an important aspect of the Old Testament faith. In the following exposition, therefore, chief stress is laid upon the comparative material. The question of the relation of word and event in Israelite ideas of revelation has not only received more attention in recent research, it is also, as I have indicated above, a separate problem which would demand a separate inquiry. Here it will be only briefly considered in my concluding remarks.

---

[13] '„Offenbarung" im Alten Testament. Ein Gespräch mit R. Rendtorff', *EvTh* 22, 1962, pp. 15 ff.

[14] 'Wolfhart Pannenberg und das Alte Testament', *NZSTh* 7, 1965, pp. 174 ff.

[15] 'Revelation Through History in the Old Testament and in Modern Theology' *Interpretation* 17, 1963, pp. 193 ff. See also the chapter on 'The Concepts of History and Revelation' in his recent book *Old and New in Interpretation. A study of the Two Testaments*, London 1966, pp. 65 ff.

CHAPTER ONE

The Divine Sphere of Activity

The gods of the Sumerian and Akkadian pantheon are to a considerable extent originally representations of the forces and elements of nature: Enlil, the 'Lord Wind', is a storm-god, Enki (Ea), the lord of the subterranean primeval ocean, is the god of the waters, Sin is the moon-god and Shamash the sun-god, Adad the weather-god with the lightning, etc. And it is obvious that the maintenance of the life of nature was a central concern in the polytheistic cults in the ancient Near East. In a sense the following characterization of the ancient polytheist and his religion is justified: 'Nature was the indigenous realm of the superhuman, and the forces of nature were the gods he worshipped.'[1]

Yet it is easy to draw a wrong inference from the fact that the gods of the ancient Near East may justly be called nature-gods. This knowledge sometimes leads to the conclusion, often drawn instinctively and almost unwittingly, that their only sphere of activity is necessarily nature or that particular realm of nature with which they are closely associated. This may be a very natural inference, but it is nevertheless mistaken. The activities of the so-called nature-gods are by no means restricted to what we call nature.[2] There are a great many texts to show that they were believed to have power over other spheres of life

---

[1] Wright, *God Who Acts*, p. 39. Cf. the same author's *The Old Testament Against Its Environment* (SBT 2), London 1950, pp. 16 ff., 93 ff.

[2] Cf. the similar point made by W. Robertson Smith, *Lectures on the Religion of the Semites. The Fundamental Institutions*, 3rd ed., London 1927: 'If a Semitic worshipper was sick he called upon his national or tribal god, and the same god was addressed if he desired rain or victory over enemies. The power of a god was not conceived as unlimited, but it was very great, and applied to all sorts of things that men could desire. So far as primitive Semitic heathenism is concerned, it is quite a mistake to suppose that a god to whom men prayed for rain was necessarily a god of clouds, while another deity was the god of flocks, and the proper recipient of prayers of increase in the sheepfold.' (p. 82). 'To say that a god who can make rain is necessarily an elemental power associated with the clouds and the sky, is as absurd as to say that Hera was the goddess of Love when she borrowed the girdle of Aphrodite. This is a very obvious remark, but it knocks on the head a great deal that has been written about Semitic religion.' (p. 83).

as well, and history is one section of that manifold reality which the gods are thought to control.

Enlil is a case in point.[3] Like other Mesopotamian deities he is originally an embodiment of a force of nature; his element is the devastating storm. But his sphere of activity is not identical with that of the wind as a natural phenomenon. His overwhelming power is turned against the enemies of his country; it is he who brings about their defeat. His terrifying wrath may also be directed against his own city: the calamities and destructions which befall it are ultimately not the achievement of the enemy but a result of Enlil's anger. He is a god who acts also in history. His character has been described in terms which read in fact exactly like a description of the Israelite Yhwh: 'There is hardly anything, with the possible exception of the nether world, which does not somehow belong to Enlil's sphere of action.'[4]

Many other Mesopotamian 'nature-gods' have, like Enlil, a sort of omnipotence which includes the power over historical events. There is ample evidence for this belief, in numerous texts from widely different periods of Mesopotamian history.

It is evident already in the earliest instances of boundary stones and building inscriptions, both of which contain curses directed against all who violate the decrees or who deface the name of the builder. In these inscriptions, from the oldest examples down to specimens from later ages, we meet the wish that transgressors and vandals should suffer misfortunes in all spheres of life, within both nature and history, and the gods who are invoked to fulfil these desires are thought to reign over all these domains.

A very old instance of these types of inscriptions is a Sumerian text, which S. N. Kramer dates in about 2400 B.C.[5] 'Its primary purpose is to record the restoration of the boundary ditch between Lagash and Umma, which had been destroyed in the course of the most recent struggle between the two cities.'[6] This boundary is said to be in accordance with the will of the gods, and in the concluding lines of the inscrip-

---

[3] See F. Nötscher, *Ellil in Sumer und Akkad*, Hannover 1927, pp. 45 ff.

[4] Nötscher, op. cit., p. 55: 'Es gibt also, etwa von der Unterwelt . . . abgesehen, kaum etwas, das nicht irgendwie in den Wirkungsbereich Ellils fiele.'

[5] S. N. Kramer, 'Sumerian Historiography', *IEJ* 3, 1953, p. 219. Kramer uses the so-called 'short chronology' (op. cit., p. 220, n. 4), on which see e.g. W. F. Albright, 'A Third Revision of the Early Chronology of Western Asia', *BASOR* 88, 1942, pp. 28 ff.; 'An Indirect Synchronism Between Egypt and Mesopotamia, cir. 1730 B.C.', *BASOR* 99, 1945, pp. 9 ff.; *From the Stone Age to Christianity. Monotheism and the Historical Process*, 2nd ed., Baltimore 1946, p. 364.

[6] Kramer, op. cit., p. 221.

tion a terrible curse is invoked on everybody who trespasses on territory belonging to Lagash:

> The Ummaite who (at any future time) will cross the boundary ditch of Ningirsu (and) the boundary ditch of Nanshe in order to take to himself fields and farms by force, whether he be (really) an Ummaite or a foreigner—may Enlil destroy him; may Ningirsu, after hurling his great Shush-net on him, bring down on him his lofty hand (and) his lofty foot; may the people of his city, having risen in rebellion, strike him down in the midst of his city.[7]

These gods are not seen as mere elemental forces but as beings capable of punishing a transgressor and causing political unrest against him.[8]

Such curses are especially common towards the end of building inscriptions, where they recur with an almost tiring monotony: they constitute a very fixed element in this *Gattung*. A few examples must suffice.

One of the many inscriptions of the Assyrian king Tukulti-Ninurta I (13th century B.C.) records the building of the city Kar-Tukulti-Ninurta with a temple for Assur and its *ziqqurrat*.[9] The text concludes with an exhortation to a future king to restore the temple and its tower, should they have fallen into decay. If he rebuilds the sanctuary and performs the customary rites, the gods will grant his petitions, but Tukulti-Ninurta invokes the most terrible curses on any successor who obliterates the inscription with his name and fails to take care of the buildings (ll. 135 ff.):[10]

... ^{d}aš-šur ^{d}enlil ù ^{d}šá-maš ilâni^{meš}	... may Ashur, Enlil and Shamash,
tik-lu-ja i-na ta-ni-ḫi ù lu-mu-un	the gods, my helpers, lead him
lìb-bi li-ir-te-du-uš e-em qa-ab-li	in pain and affliction of heart,

---

[7] The translation quoted is that given by Kramer, op. cit., p. 226. It is a 'literal translation' (ibid., p. 224). The text was published already by F. Thureau-Dangin in *Die sumerischen und akkadischen Königsinschriften* (VAB I: 1), Leipzig 1907, pp. 36 ff. The passage quoted above is found on p. 40 (transliteration) and p. 41 (German translation).

[8] The rebellion mentioned in the inscription is not explicitly said to be caused by the gods, but the context makes this interpretation natural, especially as the text as a whole 'constantly interweaves the deeds of men and gods and often fails to distinguish between them.' (Kramer, op. cit., p. 221). Cf. also the comment by R. G. Collingwood: the events 'are conceived in the first instance not as human actions but as divine actions', (*The Idea of History*, Oxford 1946, pp. 11 f.).

[9] E. Weidner, *Die Inschriften Tukulti-Ninurtas I. und seiner Nachfolger* (AfO Beiheft 12), Graz 1959, pp. 26 ff., (inscription no. 16).

[10] Ll. 119 ff. (Weidner, op. cit., p. 29).

ù ta-ḫa-zi ^{iš}*kakkê*^{meš}*-šu lu-šab-be-ru a-bi-ik-tu ummânâ*^{meš-te}*-šu liš-ku-nu a-na qât šarri bêl li-mut-ti-šu lu-me-el-lu-šu-ma i-na mât nakirê*^{meš}*-šu ka-mi-iš lu-šá-ši-bu-uš šarrū-su lis-ki-pu šùm-šu ù zêr-šu i-na ma-a-ti lu-ḫal-li-qu*

in all fights and battles[11] may they break his weapons, bring about the defeat of his troops, may they extradite him to an enemy king, in the land of his adversaries may they make him imprisoned, his kingship may they overthrow, his name and his seed may they destroy in the country.

Obviously these curses presuppose a belief in the gods' ability to govern all domains of life and to act in history as well as in nature: most of the afflictions invoked on the negligent ruler are political and military disasters. But it is not a question of specialized functions: of the three gods mentioned, neither Enlil nor Shamash are at all typical war gods. They belong to the group of deities which is usually characterized as originally personifications of natural phenomena (in this case the storm and the sun), but this does not in the least prevent them from being active in human affairs.

Similar passages are found in other building inscriptions by Tukulti-Ninurta I himself[12] and by other Mesopotamian kings.[13] These Akkadian curses may be compared with the curses invoked on an apostate people in Deut. 28.15 ff., where the divine wrath threatens Israel's entire existence in a very similar way:[13a] the punishment includes pestilence, failure of the crops, famine, military defeats and political oppression. The same conceptions of divine activities in all spheres of life are presupposed in the curses which often conclude other ancient Near Eastern texts of similar types. A well-known example is the long series of curses in the epilogue of the Code of Hammurapi; they occur fre-

---

[11] For this translation see von Soden, *AHw*, s.v. *ēm*.

[12] See e.g. Weidner, op. cit., inscription no. 5, ll. 94 ff. (p. 13); inscription no. 15, ll. 59 ff. (pp. 25 f.).

[13] See e.g. E. Ebeling–B. Meissner–E. F. Weidner, *Die Inschriften der altassyrischen Könige* (AOB 1), Leipzig 1926, pp. 24 ff. (Shamshi-Adad I, c. 1800 B.C.), 64 ff. (Adad-nirari I, c. 1300 B.C.), 124 ff. (Shalmaneser I, 13th century B.C.); R. Borger, *Die Inschriften Asarhaddons Königs von Assyrien* (AfO Beiheft 9), Graz 1956, pp. 6, 28 f. (7th century B.C.).

[13a] Cf. also the marked resemblance between the curses in the *adê*-texts of Esarhaddon (published by D. J. Wiseman, 'The Vassal-Treaties of Esarhaddon', *Iraq* 20, 1958, pp. 1 ff.) and Deut. 28.15 ff.: see R. Frankena, 'The Vassal-Treaties of Esarhaddon and the Dating of Deuteronomy', כה *1940–1965* (OTS 14), Leiden 1965, pp. 122 ff.

quently also in Hittite treaties,[14] as well as in the Babylonian *kudurrus* (boundary stones) and memorial tablets.[14a] A stone tablet engraved with the record of Nabu-apla-iddina's re-endowment of the sun-temple at Sippar and published by L. W. King[15] contains a representative example. At the end of the inscription there is a solemn warning addressed against anybody who may be bold enough to annul the gift of king Nabu-apla-iddina, to present it to another, to make deductions from the allowances, or to destroy the tablet (col. VI, ll. 45 ff.):[16]

amêlu šu-a-tum ina a-mat ^d*šamaš*	. . . as for that man by the
^d*aja u* ^d*bu-ne-ne bêlê*^{meš} *purussî*	command of Shamash, Aya and
ilâni^{meš} *rabûti*^{meš} *šum-šu liḫ-liq*	Bunene, lords of the decision, the
lil-la-qit zêr-šu ina un-ṣi u bubûti	great gods, may his name perish,
na-piš-tuš liq-ti lim-qut šal-mat-	may his seed be destroyed,
su-ma qé-bé-ra a-a ir-ši	may his life come to an end, may
	his corpse be cast aside (lit., fall
	down) and may he have no burial!

amêlu šu-a-tum ina a-mat ^d*šamaš*
^d*aja u* ^d*bu-ne-ne bêlê*^{meš} *purussî*
ilâni^{meš} *rabûti*^{meš} *šum-šu liḫ-liq*
lil-la-qit zêr-šu ina un-ṣi u bubûti
na-piš-tuš liq-ti lim-qut šal-mat-
su-ma qé-bé-ra a-a ir-ši

Here again the divine retribution is thought to affect the offender in many different areas, and the activities of the gods are clearly not restricted to what we call nature. The events which the gods are supposed to bring about are also historical events.

The same is true of a passage from a wholly different branch of ancient literature, a state letter:[17]

---

[14] See, e.g., E. F. Weidner, *Politische Dokumente aus Kleinasien. Die Staatsverträge in akkadischer Sprache aus dem Archiv von Boghazköi* (Boghazköi-Studien 8), Leipzig 1923, pp. 26 ff. (a treaty between Suppiluliumas and Mattiwaza, king of Mitanni) and *passim*. A few of these treaties are translated in *ANET*[2], pp. 201 ff. Cf. also J. Friedrich, *Staatsverträge des Hatti-Reiches in hethitischer Sprache*, 1–2 (MVAG 31: 1; 34: 1), Leipzig 1926–30, *passim*. In the texts published by Friedrich it is often said that the oaths will destroy the one who violates the treaty (e.g. pp. 24 f.); this is however probably an abridged mode of expression: the real agents are the gods who are witnesses to the treaty and to the oaths. Another possible explanation is that put forward by Friedrich, *Aus dem hethitischen Schrifttum. Übersetzungen von Keilschrifttexten aus dem Archiv von Boghazköi*, 2 (AO 25: 2), Leipzig 1925, p. 17, n. 4: 'Die Eide sind als Gottheiten personifiziert gedacht.'

[14a] For a discussion of these curse formulas with very full examples see G. Widengren, *The Akkadian and Hebrew Psalms of Lamentation as Religious Documents. A Comparative Study*, Stockholm 1937, pp. 292 ff.

[15] *Babylonian Boundary-Stones and Memorial-Tablets in the British Museum*, London 1912, pp. 120 ff. Nabu-apla-iddina reigned in the 9th century B.C.

[16] Col. VI, ll. 45 ff. (King, op. cit., pp. 126 f.).

[17] R. H. Pfeiffer, *State Letters of Assyria. A Transliteration and Translation of 355 Official Assyrian Letters dating from the Sargonid Period (722–625 B.C.)* (AOS 6), New Haven 1935, pp. 23 f., letter no. 26, ll. 6 ff. (=R. F. Harper, *Assyrian and*

ᵐú-pa-qu šá šarru bêl-a iš-pu-ra
it-tan-nu-nu ᵈbêl ù ᵈnabû ᵈištar
uruk^{ki} ù ᵈna-na-a ul-tu și-it ᵈšámši^{ši}
a-di e-rib ᵈšámši^{ši} lu-qat-tu-ma
a-na šarri bêli-ia lid-di-nu ù
šarrâni^{meš} šá nap-ḫar mâtâti a-na
pa-ni ^{[giš]}kakki šá šarri bêli-ia
lu-šak-ni-šú

As to Upaqu, about whom the king my lord has written: they have given him to me. Bel, Nabu, Ishtar of Erech and Nana may from the sunrise to the sunset utterly destroy him and deliver (him) into the hands of the king my lord; the kings of all countries may they bring into subjection before the weapons of the king my lord.

The letter was written by an official named Kudurru, who lived during the reign of Ashurbanipal,[18] i.e. in the middle of the 7th century B.C. It is interesting to note how the malediction of Upaqu is reminiscent of the curses in the building inscriptions and memorial tablets quoted above; it would almost seem as if this age-old *Gattung* had influenced the writer of this official letter. Upaqu is otherwise unknown and cannot have been too important; it is strange that he is cursed in such world-wide terms. The belief in the gods' ability to intervene everywhere and to govern also the course of historical events is at any rate the same here as in the inscriptions. It is evident not only from the curse in this text but also from the wishes for the prosperity of the king: the divine blessing is believed to assume the form of a military victory, which is especially said to be caused by the gods. It is of course to be expected that not only curses but also blessings should express this idea: if the god has power to punish offenders by sending misfortunes and calamities, he is also able to favour the righteous with prosperity and success in all their undertakings. This is the presupposition underlying the following prayer by Tiglath-Pileser I (c. 1100 B.C.). It is found in a long cylinder inscription[19] giving a detailed description of the king's campaigns and ending with an account of the rebuilding of the temple of Anu and Adad. In return for this pious deed the king asks for the favours of the two gods (col. VIII, ll. 23 ff.):[20]

Babylonian Letters, Chicago 1892–1914, no. 277; translated also by L. Waterman, *Royal Correspondence of the Assyrian Empire,* Ann Arbor 1930–36, under the same number).

[18] Pfeiffer, op. cit., p. 248.

[19] E. A. W. Budge–L. W. King, *Annals of the Kings of Assyria. The Cuneiform Texts with Translations, Transliterations, etc., from the Original Documents in the British Museum,* I, London 1902, pp. 27 ff.

[20] Op. cit., pp. 102 f. A translation is also found in D. D. Luckenbill, *Ancient Records of Assyria and Babylonia,* I, Chicago 1926, pp. 89 f., § 263.

ᵈa-nu ù ᵈadad ki-niš li-saḫ-ru-ni-ma	. . . may Anu and Adad truly turn
ni-iš qa-ti-ia li-ra-mu te-me-eq	unto me, may they take pleasure
ik-ri-be-ia liš-me-ú zu-ú-ni	in the lifting up of my hand, may
ṭa-aḫ-du-te ša-na-at nu-uḫ-še ù	they give ear unto my fervent
maš-re-e a-na palê-ia liš-ru-ku i-na	supplication. Copious rains, and
qabli u ta-ḫa-zi šal-miš lit-tar-	years of abundance and plenty
ru-ú-ni nap-ḫar mâtâtiᵐᵉˢ	during my reign may they grant.
nakirêᵐᵉˢ-ia mâtâtiᵐᵉˢ šap-ṣu-te	In battle and combat may they
ù mal-kiᵐᵉˢ za-e-ri-ia a-na	lead me in safety. All the lands of
šêpêᵐᵉˢ-ia lu-ú-šek-ni-šu	my enemies, the lands of rulers
	and princes who hate me may
	they bring into submission under
	my feet.

Tiglath-Pileser here puts together the world of nature and the world of
history. Both are seen as provinces of the same divine kingdom in
precisely the same manner as in Isaac's blessing in the Old Testament:

ויתן־לך האלהים מטל השמים	May God give you of the dew of
ומשמני הארץ ורב דגן ותירש:	heaven, and of the fatness of the
יעבדוך עמים וישתחו לך לאמים	earth, and plenty of corn and
הוה גביר לאחיך וישתחוו לך	wine. Let peoples serve you, and
בני אמך	nations bow down to you. Be lord
	over your brothers, and may your
	mother's sons bow down to you.
	(Gen. 27.28 f.)[21]

or as in the psalmist's exhortation to praise Yhwh:

כי־חזק בריחי שעריך	For he strengthens the bars of your gates;
ברך בניך בקרבך:	he blesses your children within you.
השם־גבולך שלום	He makes peace in your borders;
חלב חטים ישביעך:	he fills you with the finest of the wheat.
	(Ps. 147.13 f.)

Yhwh's dominion includes both history and nature, 'his kingdom rules
over all', מלכותו בכל משלה (Ps. 103.19). The two deities mentioned in
the Assyrian prayer are the high god Anu, a sky god, and the storm god
Adad. Not only the vegetation and the harvest are their concern: they
also rule over the world of military and political events, the domain of

---

[21] Cf. the blessings in Deut. 28.1 ff., which also presuppose that Yhwh's sphere of
activity includes both nature and history.

history.[22] All that happens is controlled and governed by divine powers —that is the basic belief. The idea of a divine rule in what we call history seems to be a simple corollary to the general belief in divine omnipotence.

It seems clear, then, that the gods of the ancient Near East were supposed to reign over a realm which included the two spheres which we call nature and history (but which may not have been clearly distinguished at all by those who worshipped these gods). Even the 'nature-gods' obviously had something to do with historical events,[23] and it seems therefore reasonable to ask what relations the gods were thought to have to history and to attempt to get a more detailed picture of these relations. We must examine what the texts disclose about this. Historical texts of course must play a prominent part, but other genres must be considered as well. The selections of texts will have to be fairly full, at the peril of being somewhat monotonous; only so can the risk of an arbitrary and one-sided picture, based on slender evidence, be avoided.

---

[22] To say that Tiglath-Pileser here speaks of the realms of nature and history in one breath is, perhaps, slightly misleading: it may be more correct to conclude that the very distinction between nature and history, so self-evident to us, is alien to this prayer, as indeed to all texts quoted above. Cf. H. and H. A. Frankfort in H. Frankfort *et al.*, *The Intellectual Adventure of Ancient Man. An Essay on Speculative Thought in the Ancient Near East*, Chicago 1946, p. 4: in the ancient Near East 'the realm of nature and the realm of man were not distinguished.' For the biblical material see also the interesting comments by F. G. Downing, *Has Christianity a Revelation?*, London 1964, pp. 244 ff.

[23] This is true already at an early stage of Mesopotamian religion: cf. T. Jacobsen's description of the situation in the third millennium: 'The gods, seen as kings and rulers, were no longer powers in nature only, they became powers in human affairs —in history.' ('Ancient Mesopotamian Religion: the Central Concerns', *PAPhS* 107, 1963, p. 479).

CHAPTER TWO

Historical Events as Divine Actions

That historical events were interpreted as divine actions is evident
already in very early Sumerian tablets. A text which has long attracted
the interest of scholars because of its importance as a testimony of the
Sumerian view of history is the composition commonly called 'The
Curse of Akkad', recently republished by A. Falkenstein on the basis
of many new tablets and fragments.[1] It is now known in numerous
copies, some of them quite extensive. There are however still several
passages of the text which are uncertain,[2] though its principal contents
are clear. All the 27 texts used by Falkenstein for his edition are from
the Old Babylonian period and all come from Nippur.[3] The composition
is not a lamentation over the destruction of Akkad, as its beginning
would seem to indicate and as was also previously believed. The text is
rather to be described as 'a historiographic document written in a highly
poetic prose';[4] this is now clear from the texts of the Hilprecht Collection in Jena, which allow the second half of the composition to be
almost completely restored.

The composition begins with a description of the period of prosperity
for the city of Akkad which had begun under its famous king Sargon
(Sharrumkin). Enlil had invested him with *en*-ship (lordship) and
kingship, and he had destroyed the power of Kish and Uruk. The
goddess Inanna built the 'house' of Akkad, i.e. her temple, filled it with
precious things and granted unto the inhabitants all the blessings of
this life. Naramsin, the ruling king of Akkad, is likened to a radiant sun,
and we hear how the power and glory of his capital were acknowledged

---

[1] 'Fluch über Akkade', *ZA* 57 (N.F. 23), 1965, pp. 43 ff. Cf. the previous edition by
H. G. Güterbock in 'Die historische Tradition und ihre literarische Gestaltung bei
Babyloniern und Hethitern bis 1200', *ZA* 42 (N.F. 8), 1934, pp. 24 ff. (there called
'der grosse Naramsin-Text'), and see also S. N. Kramer, *From the Tablets of Sumer*,
Indian Hills 1956, pp. 267 ff.

[2] Falkenstein, op. cit., p. 44 ("... an vielen Stellen wegen der Unsicherheit der
Kopien kein zweifelsfreier Text ...").

[3] Op. cit., p. 45.

[4] Kramer, op. cit., p. 267.

by foreign peoples, who brought their treasures into Akkad.

But a change occurred, which seems to have brought this splendid power to a sudden end. The tutelary goddess left her shrine in Akkad and turned her weapons against her own city:

> Aus der Stadt ging sie weg, sie, die dort wohnte,
> wie ein junges Mädchen, das ihr Frauengemach verlässt,
> verliess die heilige Inanna das 'Haus' (von) Akkade.
> Wie ein Held, der zu den Waffen eilt,
> zog sie aus gegen die Stadt zu Kampf (und) Schlacht,
> als ob sie feindliche Menschen schlüge, g[ing]? sie gegen ihre
> (d.i. der Stadt) Brust an.[5]

The immediate circumstances of this sudden disaster remain obscure, and this part of the text still raises many problems. After some badly damaged lines there is a passage describing how Naramsin consulted an oracle to obtain permission to build on Ekur, Enlil's great sanctuary in Nippur. After several vain attempts to get an affirmative answer he changed his mind and decided to attack Enlil's shrine and destroy it:

> Sein Verhalten zu ändern,
> Enlil gegenüber änderte er, was er (d.i. Narāmsuen) gesagt hatte,
> was er für ihn[6] unterworfen hatte, zerstreute er ihm,
> seine Truppe bot er auf.[7]

The text goes on to describe how the buildings were demolished with axes and hatchets and how the temple was desecrated and plundered and all its treasures carried off to Akkad.

This sacrilege excited Enlil's fury and he brought down the wild Gutians from their mountains to destroy Akkad and avenge his temple:

> Der Sturm, der alles übertönt, der dem Land Sumer insgesamt
> gesetzt ist,
> die aufspringende Flut, die keinen Widerpart hat,

---

[5] Ll. 60 ff.; Falkenstein, op. cit., p. 67. As I am myself unable to read the original text, I find it best not to attempt an English version of Falkenstein's rendering but to retain his German formulations, translations from Sumerian being notoriously difficult, often showing differences between one scholar and another. The same applies to other Sumerian texts quoted in the following and also, for the same reasons, to the Hittite texts.

[6] I.e. for Enlil; the wording here presupposes the idea that the king conducts his campaign in the service of his divine lord: cf. Falkenstein, op. cit., p. 93, and see further below, ch. 3.

[7] Ll. 100 ff.; op. cit., p. 68.

Enlil, richtete, weil sein geliebtes Ekur zerstört worden war — was
   sollte es (noch) zerstören, ...?! —
seinen Blick zum Bergland, dem feindlichen Land.
Vom weiten Gebirge liess er sie insgesamt he[rabkommen],
sie, die keinem (sonst bekannten) Volk gleichen, die nicht zu den
   Völkern gerechnet werden,
die Gutäer, die nicht wie ein (rechtes) Volk Bindungen kennen,
die (zwar) die Gestalt von Menschen (besitzen), deren Worte
   (aber) von der Beschaffenheit (der Stimme) eines Hundes sind,
liess Enlil aus dem Bergland herabkommen.
Massen (über) Massen bedeckten wie Heuschrecken die Erde.[8]

There follows a description of the ravages of the Gutians and their
fateful consequences for the whole country. In this desperate situation
eight of the great gods of the Sumerian pantheon—Sin, Enki, Inanna,
Ninurta, Ishkur, Utu, Nusku and Nisaba[9]—intervene to 'cool Enlil's
heart'; in a prayer to Enlil they pronounce a curse upon Naramsin's
city: the fate which Akkad had inflicted on Nippur shall now befall
Akkad itself:

Damals sprachen Suen, Enki, Inanna, Ninurta, Iškur, Utu, Nusku
   und Nisaba, die [gross]en Götter,
um das Herz Enlils zu 'kühlen', von selbst
zu ihm das Gebet:
„Enlil, die Stadt, die deine Stadt zerstört hat, möge wie deine Stadt
   werden, . . .“[10]

This prayer is repeated once more, and the eight deities give a detailed
list of all the disasters which are to come upon Akkad. The text then
describes how these curses came true, and it ends with a line of praise
to Inanna for the destruction of Akkad:

Dafür, [dass] Akkade vernichtet worden ist, sei Inanna Preis![11]

---

[8] Ll. 151 ff.; op. cit., p. 70.
[9] Both the consecutive order of the gods (which is the same in l. 212 and in l. 225)
and their number—eight instead of seven—are unusual; cf. Falkenstein, op. cit.,
p. 112.
[10] Ll. 212 ff.; op. cit., p. 72.
[11] L. 283; op. cit., p. 75. Falkenstein thinks it surprising that Inanna is credited with
the destruction of the city, as it is after all Enlil who is said to have summoned the
Gutians (op. cit., p. 124). The Gutian ravages however did not primarily affect
Akkad but the country as a whole, and it is because of this general devastation that
Inanna and the other gods intervene and curse Akkad, the destruction of which is
then described. This would seem to provide some justification for the concluding
line, though admittedly some difficulties still remain.

Falkenstein has shown that the narrative contains historical mistakes; first and foremost the destruction of Akkad cannot very well have occurred during the reign of Naramsin but must—to judge from primary sources—have taken place somewhat later.[12] Thus the text cannot quite simply be used as a historical source. But of course this does not detract from its great value as a source of knowledge about the Sumerian idea of history: it gives us firsthand information about how the Sumerian author pictured the relations between the gods and historical events, even if some of these events should happen to be wrongly dated.

The text bears testimony to the belief that historical events are in one way or another caused by supernatural agents, that the gods create history. The idea that their main sphere of activity is nature does not even begin to emerge: here they are all concerned with what happens in the relations of states and men. Enlil gives kingship to Sargon of Akkad; the attacks of an enemy are described as the hostile action of the goddess Inanna; the Gutian invasion is Enlil's doing, and Akkad lies waste and desolate because of a divine curse. Ancient Near Eastern interpretation of historical events in terms of divine actions[13] is thus found already in this very old text, which may reasonably be dated in the Ur III period,[14] i.e. in the last century of the third millennium B.C. This idea can then be followed down through the centuries and found in texts of very diverse character and different origin.

The famous Sumerian 'Lamentation over the Destruction of Ur'[15] is the longest specimen of this *Gattung* that has been preserved in its entirety. Ur had been made into ruins through the attacks of the Subarians and the Elamites,[16] and this catastrophe is represented in the lamentation as the work of divine powers, who used the foreign invaders as their instruments. The goddess Ningal is said to have made two attempts to placate Anu and Enlil, who had decreed the destruction of Ur. But in vain: the decision, for which no reason is given, was carried through, and Ningal laments:

---

[12] Op. cit., pp. 47 f., against Kramer, who seems to accept the statements in the text.
[13] Of course the text is also evidence of the interpretation of disasters as divine punishment and so a revelation of divine wrath; on this see further below, ch. 6.
[14] So Falkenstein, op. cit., pp. 49 f.
[15] Translations of this text have been published by among others Falkenstein in A. Falkenstein–W. von Soden, *Sumerische und akkadische Hymnen und Gebete*, Zürich-Stuttgart 1953, pp. 192 ff., and by Kramer in *ANET²*, pp. 455 ff. The translation quoted here is that of Kramer.
[16] The text gives the impression that it is a historical event which is bewailed, but the destruction of Ur described in the composition cannot be identified with the fall of Ur III under Ibbisin quite as easily as Kramer seems to believe (op. cit., p. 455): cf. the comment by Falkenstein, op. cit., p. 377.

> The utter destruction of my city verily they directed,
> the utter destruction of Ur verily they directed.[17]

The whole composition testifies to the belief that what happened in history was not in the last analysis the work of human powers but of divine. 'The utter destruction of the city was wrought, in our terms, by the barbaric hordes which attacked it. Not so in terms of the Mesopotamian's own understanding of his universe: the wild destructive essence manifest in this attack was Enlil's. The enemy hordes were but a cloak, an outward form under which that essence realized itself. In a deeper, truer sense the barbaric hordes were a storm, Enlil's storm, wherewith the god himself was executing a verdict passed on Ur and its people by the assembly of the gods; and as that storm the enemy attack is seen and described.'[18]

On a large tablet, containing copies of inscriptions from the temple Ekur in Nippur, we find the following lines in a bilingual statue inscription of Sargon of Akkad:[19]

⌐sar-ru-GI⌐ [LU]G[AL] in	Sargon, the king, prostrated him-
tu-tu-li^KI a-na ^dda-gan uš-ga-en	self before (the god) Dagan in
ik-ru-ub ma-d⌐am⌐ a-li-dam	Tutul and prayed. He gave him
i(erasure)-ti-šum ma-ri-am^KI	the Upper Region (i.e.) Mari,
ì-ar-mu-ti-a-am^KI eb-la^KI a-ti-ma	Iarmuti (and) Ebla as far as the
⌐GIŠ.TIR⌐ ⌐GIŠ.ERIN⌐ ù	Cedar Forest and the Silver
KUR.KUR KÙ	Mountains.

And in another text on the same tablet, an inscription on the pedestal of a statue of Sargon, it says:[20]

[sar-ru-GI] ša[r] (LUG[AL])	Enlil did [not let anybody ri]val
mâtim (⌐KALAM⌐.MA.[KI])	[Sargon], the king of the country.
^d⌐en⌐-lil ma-[ḫi-ra] [la i-ti-nu-	Enlil gave him [the Upper Sea
šum] [ti-a-am-dam] [a-li-dam]	and the Lo]wer Sea.
[ù] [sa-bil]-dam ⌐d⌐en-lil	
i-ti-nu-šum	

---

[17] Ll. 162 f.; *ANET*², p. 458.

[18] T. Jacobsen in H. Frankfort *et al.*, *The Intellectual Adventure of Ancient Man*, p. 141.—Possibly Jacobsen is here laying too much stress on Enlil's character as a storm-god (cf. p. 142: 'In the great catastrophes of history, in the crushing blows voted by the assembly of the gods, there is Enlil, essence of the storm'): what is here attributed to Enlil is in other texts in fact said about deities who are *not* storm-gods.

[19] H. Hirsch, 'Die Inschriften der Könige von Agade', *AfO* 20, 1963, p. 38 (the inscription 'Sargon b 2', ll. 17 ff.); for a duplicate see p. 49 ('Sargon b 13'). Cf. G. A. Barton, *The Royal Inscriptions of Sumer and Akkad* (Library of Ancient Semitic Inscriptions, I), New Haven 1929, pp. 108 f.

[20] Hirsch, op. cit., p. 36 ('Sargon b 1', col. 4, ll. 1 ff.). Cf. Barton, op. cit., pp. 104 f.

Sargon reigned c. 2300 B.C. and the tablet with the copies of his inscriptions seems to have been written soon after his dynasty had been overthrown about a century and a half later.[21] In these ancient texts it is quite clear that the god is not exclusively regarded as a god of nature. The conquered territories are seen as his gift,[22] and the king reigns without opposition because this is the god's will. The author of these lines had traced divine powers not only behind the forces of nature: in political events too he found the will and domination of his god.

Sargon's grandson Naramsin is the hero of an ancient document belonging to a *Gattung* which Güterbock has called *'narû*-Literatur'.[23] A *narû* is a royal stele with an inscription in the first person, recording the events of the king's reign and usually ending with the traditional curses and blessings.[24] What Güterbock calls *'narû*-literature' is a number of texts, cast in the form of such a royal inscription but pseudepigraphic, with a legendary content and a strong didactic colouring. The matter is often taken from the traditions about the kings of Akkad; the well-known legend of he birth of Sargon is a typical example. To this group belongs also the composition now called 'The Cuthaean Legend of Naram-Sin' (several different names have previously been suggested by editors of fragments of this text). Parts of it were published by Güterbock.[25] The first edition of the whole text in its proper sequence has been prepared by O. R. Gurney[26] on the basis of more recent material, above all a newly discovered tablet from Sultantepe, which revealed that fragments previously held to be parts of different compositions did in fact belong to this legend. 'The text is still incomplete and many problems remain to be solved',[27] but the content is clear at least in its chief outlines. The interesting thing in this document from our point of view is its tendency. Güterbock thought that it preached the moral 'Alle Mühe ist vergeblich!'[28] but the more complete version now shows this to be somewhat inadequate as a summing up: instead

---

[21] A. L. Oppenheim in *ANET²*, p. 267. Hirsch calls these copies 'Altbabylonische Abschriften', op. cit., p. 2.

[22] This is by no means an isolated instance: about a millennium later, for instance, Tukulti-Ninurta I speaks about the borderland districts subjugated by him as the gift of the great gods: Weidner, *Die Inschriften Tukulti-Ninurtas I.*, pp. 4 f. (inscription no. 1, col. IV, ll. 24 ff.).

[23] Güterbock, op. cit., pp. 19; 62 ff.

[24] Cf. above, pp. 18 ff.

[25] Op. cit., pp. 69 ff.

[26] 'The Sultantepe Tablets (*Continued*). IV. The Cuthaean Legend of Naram-sin', *AS* 5, 1955, pp. 93 ff.

[27] Gurney, op. cit., p. 95.

[28] Op. cit., p. 75.

the 'emphasis is on the fact that events are determined by the will of the gods rather than by the efforts of men', to quote Gurney's summary of the lesson of this text.[29] This appears from the text as a whole rather than from individual passages, but there are also a few lines which clearly express the idea of a divine control of the course of events, e.g. the words of 'the bright Venus' addressed to Naramsin, admonishing him to have mercy on his enemies and to leave revenge to the gods, who will punish them according to their desert (ll. 131 ff.):[30]

ana ár-kat u_4-me ^{d}en-líl ana lemutti^{ti} i-na-áš-šá re-su-un	In days to come Enlil will summon them for evil:
ana ag-gi lìb-bi ^{d}en-líl ú-qa-a-'-u re-e-šú	they are waiting for the angry heart of Enlil.
āl ṣābē šu-nu-ti in-⌜ne⌝-ru	The city of the warriors will be ⌜massacred⌝,
i-qam-mu-ú i-lam-mu-u šubāti (⌜KI⌝.DÚR.MEŠ)	its dwellings will be burnt and besieged.

The destruction of the enemies' city is conceived as the action of Enlil.

The Legend of Naramsin, like other texts belonging to the 'narû literature', was probably composed in the early second millennium B.C.[31] A composition narrating similar events has been published by J. J. Finkelstein.[32] It seems to be an earlier version of the legend, and the tablet on which it is written can be dated on paleographical grounds toward the end of the Old Babylonian period.[33] Finkelstein has even identified the scribe as a certain 'Ellet-Aya who worked at Sippar during the reign of Ammi-ṣaduqa',[34] i.e. in the second half of the 17th century B.C.

This text represents the same view of the true nature of historical events. After crushing defeats the king is downcast (col. III, ll. 8 ff.):[35]

a-na-ku es-si-ḫi en-ni-ši	I became confused, I was bewildered.
a-ka-ad a-na-aḫ a-šu-uš am-ṭi-ma	I despaired (?), I groaned, I grieved, I grew faint.

---

[29] Op. cit., p. 96.
[30] Op. cit., pp. 106 f.
[31] Op. cit., p. 91.
[32] 'The So-called "Old Babylonian Kutha Legend"', JCS 11, 1957, pp. 83 ff.
[33] Op. cit., p. 83.
[34] Ibid.
[35] Op. cit., p. 85.

um-ma a-na-ku-ma[36] AN *a-na*	Thus I thought: 'What has God
palê-ia mi-nam ub-lam	brought upon my reign.
a-na-ku šar-rum la mu-ša-lim	I am a king who has not kept his
ma-ti-šu	land prosperous.

As a matter of course the disaster is held to be caused by a divine power. Later on in this composition a terrible devastation is described, in which the cities are laid in ruins and the whole country laid waste. And this 'attack by the enemy horde is, in the Mesopotamian world view, only a manifestation of the wrathful god'.[37]

This view also dominates the famous Era Epic, originally named after its opening words *šar gimir dadmī*, 'King of all dwellingplaces'. It has been called 'one of the masterpieces of Akkadian epic literature'.[38] Era (or Irra), the god of pestilence, had decided to ravage and destroy Babylonia. To be able to carry out his intentions he must persuade Marduk to leave his shrine, and he contrives to make him descend into the nether world. When Marduk is away, Era lets loose devastation on Babylon and on the whole country. Temples and cities are demolished; the fourth tablet contains a long lament over the destruction of Babylon. At last Era is appeased by his vizier, the god Ishum, and in the end pronounces blessings on the stricken land and predicts its return to wealth and domination.

It seems clear that the author of this composition, whose name is mentioned in the last tablet (V. 42): Kabti-ilāni-Marduk, son of Dabibi,[39] had historical events in view when he described the ravages of Era. The fact that both invading peoples and destroyed cities are mentioned by their names provides a basis for dating the epic, though there is some disagreement about the correct evaluation of these data. Gössmann[40] suggests that geographical and ethnographical details indicate the century 722–626 B.C. and that the historical background is to be seen in events which happened during the reigns of the two Assyrian kings Sargon II (721–705) and Sennacherib (705–681). Some details seem to fit especially the later part of this period, and Gössmann in the end

---

[36] The last sign in *a-na-ku-ma* was earlier read as *šu* and the name of the king was supposed to be Šu-ili (so e.g. Güterbock, op. cit., p. 66). Finkelstein's definite establishing of the text 'finally disposes of the shadowy "Šu-ili", heretofore presumed to be the narrating ruler.' (Finkelstein, op. cit., p. 87).

[37] Op. cit., p. 87, n. 15.

[38] W. G. Lambert, '[Review of] F. Gössmann, Das Era-Epos ...', *AfO* 18, 1957–58, p. 395.

[39] Lambert, 'The Fifth Tablet of the Era Epic', *Iraq* 24, 1962, p. 123, gives the form Kabti-ilī-Marduk.

[40] F. Gössmann, *Das Era-Epos*, Würzburg n.d. [1956], pp. 85 ff.

maintains that the epic must have been written c. 685 B.C. Lambert[41] has argued for an earlier date and shown some of Gössmann's arguments to be based on erroneous interpretations of the text. 'The attacks on the cities are expressly said to be the work of the Sutû, Aramaean tribes who worked havoc in Babylonia shortly after 1100 B.C.'[42] Other details in the narrative point in the same direction, particularly a list of peoples which had to be dismissed by Gössmann as partly archaic names but which suits the eleventh century B.C. very well. Lambert thinks it possible and even probable that the epic was composed at the orders of Nabu-apla-iddina, who regarded himself as the avenger of the Sutû and had an active interest in literature, to chronicle the fall and rise of Akkad. The precise years of his reign are not known, but it falls in the ninth century B.C.

Here again we find a text which interprets historical disasters as the work of divine agents. The author seeks the reason why Babylonia had been reduced to ruins and finds it in the conviction that the havoc was the expression of a god's anger. But not only historical misfortunes were held to be caused by divine powers: the glorious future to which the author looks forward, when his ravaged and desolate country will again be densely populated and victorious, is also the work of the god, who ordains it (V: 25–28):[43]

niši[meš] māti e-ṣa-at	Let the sparse people of the
li-tu-ra ana ma-'-diš	land multiply again,
ku-ru-ú ki-i ar-ki	let short and tall alike tread
li-ba-'-u ú-ru-uḫ-šá	its road,
a-ku-ú [kur]akkadû[ki]	let crippled Akkad throw down
dan-na su-ta-a li-šam!-qit!	the mighty Sutû,
ištēn[en] sibitti	may one drive off seven like
li-bu-ku ki-ma ṣe-e-ni	sheep.

Era is a god of pestilence, and so the devastating actions described in the epic seem reasonably consistent with the god's destructive character, though already his activity in attacks by enemy hordes goes beyond his 'natural' domain as a pest-god. But in the passage quoted he even decrees prosperity and wealth—the following lines also speak of abundant crops and fertilizing waters—and again we see how a Mesopotamian deity cannot simply be explained as a personification of a certain phenomenon of nature but is regarded as a personal will exercising his

---

[41] AfO 18, 1957–58, pp. 396 ff.
[42] Op. cit., p. 397.
[43] Text published by Lambert, Iraq 24, 1962, p. 122.

influence in all spheres of life, including what we call historical events.

The hostile invasions are ultimately the manifestations of divine wrath —so much is quite clear from the text. But opinions differ as to the reasons for this heavenly anger. Both Gössmann[44] and Lambert[45] maintain that no reason at all is given in the epic: nothing but the god's whims govern the course of events. This view has been challenged by R. Frankena.[46] He points out that there are several passages which indicate that men had neglected the worship due to Era and that this sin of omission was the real ground for the god's resolve to lay waste the country. If Frankena is right—and there is much to be said for his view—we have in the narrative of Era's devastations another instance of the interpretation of historical events as divine punishment.[47] An additional argument in favour of Frankena's interpretation may be found in a passage where the same explanation seems to be given for the anger of another deity, an anger which is likewise manifested in enemy hordes invading the city of the sinners. In the fourth tablet we hear about Ishtar's wrath. It is said about the governor of the city of Uruk, 'the abode of Anu and Ishtar', *šubat* ^{d}*anim u* ^{d}*ištar*, (ll. 60 ff.):[48]

uš-šis-si-na-ti-ma par-ṣi-ši-na *i-te-t[i-iq?]*	He maltreated them and neglected (?) their rites.
^{d}*ištar i-gu-ug-ma is-sa-bu-us* *eli uruk^{ki}*	Ishtar became incensed and was angry with Uruk.
^{lú}*nakru id-kam-ma ke-e še-im* *ina pan mê^{meš} i-maš-šá-'-uš*	She levied the enemy, and like corn before water he snatched him away

The context is not entirely clear, and admittedly l. 60 might possibly picture the havoc worked by the enemy, i.e. the manifestation of the divine anger, not the cause of it; the words about Ishtar's wrath must then be taken as a kind of retrospect of the ultimate origin of the miserable situation in the city. But on the whole it seems to yield a more satisfactory interpretation and a better continuity in the narrative if we understand l. 60 as a description of that act of negligence which aroused Ishtar's anger mentioned in l. 61. This gives a natural sequence

---

[44] Op. cit., p. 62: '„Unbegründet" ist, soweit der heutige Zustand des Werkes ein Urteil gestattet, die gesamte Handlung im Era-Epos von Anfang bis zum Ende. Im Grunde ist Willkür und Laune Ursache alles Geschehens.' Cf. also p. 77.

[45] *Iraq* 24, 1962, p. 119: 'No grounds, ultimately, for this anger are suggested: it was the god's nature.'

[46] 'Het Epos van de Pestgod Irra', *JEOL* 15, 1957–58, p. 174.

[47] See further below, ch. 6.

[48] The text in Gössmann, op. cit., p. 29.

in ll. 61–63: the cause, the fact, and the result of the deity's anger.[49] And so interpreted these lines seem to give at least indirect support to Frankena's view, as the author of the epic is then familiar with the idea that a case of neglect in the field of worship could be the cause of divine wrath.

As is evident from the different quotations given above, the idea of historical events as divine actions is not restricted to a certain type of texts. Just as they come from the most different periods of ancient Mesopotamian history, so they represent also the most different categories of literature: historical texts, hymns, prayers and rituals. A lamentation included in an inscription by the famous Assyrian king Ashurbanipal (668–627 B.C.) first describes the troublesome situation in his kingdom (Clay tablet L³ (K 891), rev. ll. 6 f.):[50]

ina mâti ṣal-ta ina bîti	Fighting within (my) country
pu-uḫ-pu-uḫ-u la ip-par-ra-su	(and) bickering within (my)
idâ[^{IImeš}-a-a] du-lu-uḫ-ḫu-u	family do not stop;[51] disturbance
a-mat lemuttim^{tim} su-ud-du-ru-u-ni	(and) evil talk are constantly
ka-a-a-an	arrayed against me.

The prayer is then concluded with the following words (ll. 14 f.):

adi im-mat ilu an-na-a	How long, O God, will you do
te-ep-pu-šá-an-ni ki-i la	this to me? I am treated like
pa-li-iḫ ili ù ^{d}ištar ana-ku	one who does not fear god and
ep-ša-[ku]	goddess.

When the king here complains about discord and rebellion, he is no doubt aiming at human adversaries, but the god is regarded as the real originator of the tribulations: 'How long, O God, will you do this to me?' Of the reason nothing is said: there is not a word here about any guilt or transgression on the part of the king.[52]

There is another inscription by Ashurbanipal expressing the same

---

[49] Gössmann may be right that *two* invasions are described in this section: the city is first captured by the Sutû, whose sovereign (the šakkanakku, 'governor', of Uruk mentioned in l. 59) neglects the cult of Ishtar in the temple Eanna, with the result that the goddess is angry and summons 'the enemy', who sacks the city a second time (cf. Gössmann, op. cit., p. 79).

[50] M. Streck, *Assurbanipal und die letzten assyrischen Könige bis zum Untergange Niniveh's*, II (VAB 7: 2), Leipzig 1916, p. 252; cf. F. Delitzsch, *Assyrische Lesestücke* ... (Assyriologische Bibliothek 16), 4. Aufl., Leipzig 1900, p. 143.

[51] For this translation see *CAD* s. v. ṣaltu, p. 87 b.

[52] Cf. von Soden in Falkenstein–von Soden, *Sumerische und akkadische Hymnen und Gebete*, p. 387.

belief: that the divine powers are active in historical events. It is a large trilingual limestone inscription from the temple of Ishtar at Nineveh, found in about 120 pieces during the British excavations there in the early 1930's.[53] In ll. 76 ff. Ashurbanipal says:[54]

ilâni^meš rabûti^meš bêli^meš-i[a]
... -[šu]-nu-ti ki-niš ip-pal-su-in-ni-ma [itallaku] ida-a-a andulla^la-šu-nu ṭâba eli-ia it-r[u-ṣu-ma ip-še]-ti-ia damqâti^meš ha-diš ip-pal-su-ma ik-... šarru-u-ti mâtâti kal-ši-na ul-tu tam-tim eli-[ti] a-di tam-tim [ša]p-li-ti a-na ni-[ri-ia] u-ša[k-ni-šu

The great gods, my lords, [with] their ... looked upon me truly and [went] at my side; their kindly aegis they sp[read] over me: my good [wor]ks they beheld with joy, and blessed (?) my kingdom: the lands, all of them, from the Up[per] sea to the [Lo]wer sea unto [my yo]ke [they] caused [to yield]

Here we meet with the same idea of the motive forces in political and miltiary events as in the inscriptions of Sargon of Akkad nearly 1700 years earlier.[55] It is again found in a later passage in the same inscription, ll. 104 f.:[56]

... ^Itam-ma-ri-tu ^Ipa-'-e ^Ium-man-al-da-si [ša arka a-ha-miš?] e-pu-šu be-lut ^kurelamti^ki ša ^daššur ^dNIN.LIL [^diš]tar a-ši-bat ^uruarba-il u-šak-ši-du qa-ti iṣ-ba-tu šepê^II šarru-u-ti-ia ip-pu-šu ardu-u-ti

Tammaritu, Pa'e, Ummanaldas, [who after each other?] had carried on the rule of Elam, whom Ashur, Ninlil, (and) [Ish]tar dwelling in Arbela had caused my hand to conquer, clasped the feet of my royalty, doing homage to me.

It may be appropriate to remark here that in both these extracts from the inscription of Ashurbanipal in the temple of Ishtar at Nineveh the idea of the gods as the true authors of historical events is inherent in the very form of the language used: the deities are the subjects of causative forms of Akkadian verbs: uša[knišu 'they caused to bow down'; ušakšidu 'they caused to conquer'.

The conviction that the gods govern all that happens makes it natural

---

[53] R. C. Thompson–M. E. L. Mallowan, 'The British Museum Excavations at Nineveh, 1931–32', *AAA* 20, 1933, p. 79.
[54] Thompson, op. cit., p. 84 (text) and 93 (translation); his transcription lacks diacritical accents.—I have put the square brackets in the translation differently from Thompson, the better to correspond with the lacunae in the text.
[55] Cf. above, p. 28.
[56] Op. cit., p. 85 (text) and 94 (translation).

for the ancient Mesopotamians to pray to the gods not only for rain and rich harvests but also for political stability and a secure dominion, as for instance in a prayer to Marduk by Nebuchadnezzar II (604–562 B.C.), included in a long inscription[57] relating building enterprises of the king. These are the concluding words (col. III, ll. 52 ff.):[58]

iš-tu išid šamê a-di elât šamê e-ma	From horizon to zenith, where the
šamšu a-ṣu-ú ai i-ši na-ki-ri	sun rises, may there be no enemy,
mu-ga-al-li-ti ai ar-ši li-i-pu-ú-a	may I have no rebel[59] (against
i-na qí-ir-bi-ša a-na da-rí-a-tim	me). May my descendants in it
ṣa-al-ma-at qá-qá-dam li-bé-e-lu.	(i.e. the house built by N.) forever
	rule the blackheaded.[60]

---

[57] 'Nebukadnezar Nr 14', S. Langdon–R. Zehnpfund, *Die neubabylonischen Königsinschriften* (VAB 4), Leipzig 1912, pp. 23 ff. (description of the text); 112 ff. (transliteration).

[58] Op. cit., p. 120.

[59] Lit. 'one who frightens'.

[60] A passage from an inscription by the last king of Babylon, Nabonidus (555–539 B.C.), may possibly be relevant, though this depends on the translation of a difficult and disputed sentence. Nabonidus' basalt stele, now in Istanbul, contains a historical introduction, describing among other things an invasion by the Manda-hordes (col. II, ll. 8 ff.):

e-li-iš u šap-liš im-nu ù šu-me-lu a-bu-	Above and below, right and left he (i.e.
ba-niš is-pu-un ú-tir gi-mil-lu bâbiliki	the king of the Umman-Manda) over-
i-ri-ba tuk-te-e šar um-man-ma-an-da	whelmed like a flood storm, avenging
la a-diru ú-ša-al-pi-it eš-ri-it-sú-un ša	Babylon, taking vengeance. The king
ilâni kurSU.EDINki ka-la-šu-nù u ālāni	of the Umman-Manda without fear
pa-aṭ kurakkadi ša it-ti šar kurakkadi	destroyed the temples of all the gods of
na-ak-ru-ma la il-li-ku ri-ṣu-ut-sú	Subartu (i.e. Assyria) and the towns
ú-ša-al-pi-it-ma mé-e-si-šu-un ma-na-ma	in the territory of Akkad, which had
la i-zib ú-šah-ri-ib ma-ha-zi-šu-un	been hostile against the king of Akkad
ú-ša-ti-ir a-bu-bi-iš	and had not come to his assistance, he
(Langdon-Zehnpfund, op. cit.,	destroyed their cults and left nobody
pp. 272 ff.)	over, he laid waste their cities, he tore
	(them) down like a deluge.

The words which follow immediately after this passage are crucial: *šar bâbiliki ši-pi-ir dmarduk šá ši-il-la-ti ik-kib-šú la ú-bil qâtII-sú a-na pil-lu-de-e ilânimeš ka-la-ma.* Langdon's translation (loc. cit.) runs: 'Der König von Babylon — das Geheiss Marduks auf Demütigung erniedrigte ihn; nicht legte er seine Hände an die Weihgeschenke der Götter allesamt', but this does not seem to give satisfactory sense. A. L. Oppenheim translates (*ANET*², p. 309): 'The king of Babylon, however, for whom this sacrilegious action of Marduk was horrible, did not raise his hand against the cult(-places) of any of the great gods.' This presumably presupposes taking *šipir dmarduk ša šillati* together, interpreting *šipru* as 'work, deed' and *ša šillati* as a qualification of *šipir dmarduk*, which would yield the literal translation 'Marduk's act of sacrilege' (on *šillatu* see W. G. Lambert, *Babylonian Wisdom Literature*,

This belief that the gods act in history, which can be found in abundance in Mesopotamian texts, seems to have been common to the whole ancient Near East. There is no difficulty in adducing passages expressing this idea from the Hittite literature.

A Hittite 'Ritual before Battle'[61] seems to have as its very foundation the conviction that the events are ultimately the actions of divine powers. The Hittite gods are implored to blot out the Kashkean country (a mountainous district near the Black Sea, inhabited by tribes who often raided Hittite territory and seem to have been a perpetual source of unrest at the northern border of the Hittite kingdom),[62] and the gods of this hostile land are solemnly summoned before an assembly to hear the accusation which the Hittites bring against them—implying that it is in the end these gods who are to be held responsible for the hostile invasion which has given occasion to the ritual:[63]

> The gods of the Hatti land have done nothing against you, the gods of the Kashkean country. They have not put you under constraint. But ye, the gods of the Kashkean country, began war. Ye drove the gods of the Hatti land out of their realm and took over their realm for yourselves. The Kashkean people also began war. From the Hittites ye took away their cities and ye drove them out of their field (and) fallow and out of their vineyards.

Oxford 1960, p. 312). A similar translation has been suggested by L. Messerschmidt (*Die Inschrift der Stele Nabuna'id's, Königs von Babylon,* ... (MVG 1896: 1), Berlin 1896, pp. 26, 44): 'Der König von Babylon, das Verhalten Marduks, welches in Plünderung [bestand], schmerzte ihn, er legte seine Hand nicht an die Heiligtümer der Götter allesamt.' If this were the correct interpretation, we would here have a remarkable expression for the idea that the god is the real subject of the action: the ravages of the king of Umman-Manda described as 'Marduk's act of sacrilege'! But it is extremely doubtful if this interpretation can be upheld. J. Lewy translates (*Forschungen zur alten Geschichte Vorderasiens* (MVAG 29: 2), Leipzig 1925, pp. 81, 86): 'Der König von Babel, der Abgesandte Marduks, dem Sakrileg ein Greuel ist, legte nicht Hand an. Auf die (Ausübung der) Riten der Götter insgesamt...', taking *šipru* as 'Bote' (cf. K. Tallqvist, *Akkadische Götterepitheta* (StOr 7), Helsingforsiae 1938, p. 229). This interpretation is probably to be preferred: it is more natural to take *ša šillati ikkibšu* as an attribute to Marduk (or possibly to *šar bābili*) in the form of a relative clause. This, then, is very likely the meaning of the passage: 'But the king of Babylon, a carrier of orders (?) from Marduk, who abhors sacrilege, did not lay his hands upon the cult objects of the gods' (the translation suggested by Prof. J. Aro, to whom I am indebted for a helpful discussion of this passage).

[61] *ANET²*, pp. 354 f. (translator: A. Goetze).

[62] See O. R. Gurney, *The Hittites* (Pelican Books A 259), rev. ed., Harmondsworth 1962, p. 33, and Goetze in *ANET²*, p. 354, n. 1.

[63] *ANET²*, p. 355. On this passage see also E. O. Forrer, 'Eine Geschichte des Götterkönigtums aus dem Hatti-Reiche', *Mélanges Franz Cumont* (Annuaire de l'Institut de philologie et d'histoire orientales et slaves, IV), 2, Bruxelles 1936, p. 689.

The gods of the Hatti land and the (Hittite) people call for bloody vengeance.

There is a curious kind of parallelism here between the acts of the gods and the acts of the people ('the gods ... began war ... the ... people also began war'), but this does not seem to militate against the idea that the terrestrian war-incidents *are* also in some sense divine actions: the statement that the foreign gods 'drove the gods of the Hatti land out of their realm' is, of course, one way of describing the successful attack of the foreign hordes. And the parallel actions on two different levels, one divine and one human, are not mutually independent: there can be no doubt which is regarded as the original and which the reflection.

The same belief in the gods' frequent interventions in the field of human politics in evident in an early Hittite document, the so-called Proclamation of Telipinus,[64] a very valuable source for the history of the Hittite Old Kingdom. After a survey of the reigns of his predecessors Telipinus narrates events of his own time, and one passage runs (2.20 f.):[65]

> When at that time I, the king, came to Lawazzantiyas, Lahhas was hostile to me, and incited Lawazzantiyas to rebellion. And the gods delivered it into my hand.

The phrase which the king here uses to express the belief that the course of events was directed by the gods and that his victory over the enemies was a divine gift, 'the gods delivered it into my hand', seems to have been spread all over the ancient Near East and is found in texts from different ages and different areas. As is well known, it is frequently used in the Old Testament, as in e.g. Jos. 2.24:

ויאמרו אל־יהושע כי־נתן יהוה	And they said to Joshua, 'Truly
בידנו את־כל־הארץ וגם־נמגו	Yhwh has given into our hand all
כל־ישבי הארץ מפנינו:	the land; and moreover all the inhabitants of the land are fainthearted because of us.

---

[64] E. H. Sturtevant–G. Bechtel, *A Hittite Chrestomathy*, Philadelphia 1935, pp. 175 ff. On king Telipinus and his edict see e.g. Gurney, op. cit., pp. 24 ff. Sturtevant–Bechtel (op. cit., p. 194) date the proclamation in the middle of the 17th cent. B.C. Since then Hittite chronology has been revised, though it has not ceased to be a notoriously difficult and disputed subject. Gurney (loc. cit.) places Telipinus towards the end of the 16th cent., whereas A. Kammenhuber puts him in the middle of the 15th cent. ('Die hethitische Geschichtsschreibung', *Saeculum. Jahrbuch für Universalgeschichte* 9, 1958, p. 141).

[65] Sturtevant–Bechtel, op. cit., p. 189.

The phrase נתן ביד 'to give (deliver) into the hand (of)' used of God is especially frequent in the Deuteronomic History[66] but occurs also in other parts of the Old Testament.[67] It is also found in the Amarna letters: Tushratta, king of Mitanni, writes to Amenophis III of Egypt (tablet 17, ll. 32 ff.):[68]

ki-i ¹ᵘnakrūtu a-na mâti^ti-[ia]	When the enemies came to [my]
it-ta-al-ka ᵈtešub (IM) be-li a-na	country, Teshub, my lord, gave
qa-ti-ia id-din-šu-ma ù ad-du-uk-šu	them (lit., him) into my hand and I beat them (lit., him).

And the same mode of expression is used in the same sense also in Mesopotamia, as e.g. in a building inscription by Nebuchadnezzar II (col. III, ll. 18 ff.):[69]

ni-šim ra-ap-ša-a-tim ša ᵈmarduk	The numerous peoples, which
bé-e-la ú-ma-al-lu-ú qá-tu-ú-a a-na	Marduk, my lord, had delivered
ba-bi-lam^ki ú-ka-an-ni-iš	into my hand, I brought under Babylon's dominion

The idea of divine activities in historical events which we found in the Proclamation of Telipinus is evident also in the annals of the Hittite king Mursilis II (1339–1306 B.C.). Repeatedly the king emphasizes the gods' intervention on his behalf. The following is a characteristic extract from the introduction to the so-called 'Ten-Year-Annals' (Obv., col. I, ll. 22 ff.):[70]

> And to the Sun-goddess of Arinna, my lady, I raised my hand and spoke thus: 'Sun-goddess of Arinna, my lady, the surrounding hostile countries which called me a child and made light of me and were constantly trying to seize thy territories, O Sun-goddess of Arinna, my lady—come down, O Sun-goddess of Arinna, my lady, and smite these hostile countries for me.' And the Sun-goddess of Arinna heard my prayer and came to my aid, and in ten years

[66] Deut. 1.27; 2.24, 30; 3.2; 7.24; 20.13; 21.10; Jos. 2.24; 6.2; 7.7 etc.; Judg. 1.2, 4; 3.10, 28; 7.7, 9, 14 etc.; 1 Sam. 14.12. etc.; 1 Kings 20.13 etc. Cf. S. R. Driver, A Critical and Exegetical Commentary on Deuteronomy (ICC), 3rd ed., Edinburgh 1902, pp. LXXXII and 48 (on 3.2).
[67] E.g. Gen. 14.20; Ex. 23.31; Num. 21.2, 34; Jer. 20.5; Ez. 7.21; Ps. 106.41; Dan. 1.2; Neh. 9.27; 2 Chr. 16.8.
[68] J. A. Knudtzon, Die El-Amarna-Tafeln ..., 1 (VAB 2: 1), Leipzig 1907, p. 132.
[69] 'Nebukadnezar Nr. 9', Langdon–Zehnpfund, op. cit., pp. 19 f. (description of the text); 88 ff. (transliteration). Col. III is found on p. 94.
[70] Goetze, Die Annalen des Muršiliš (MVAG 38), Leipzig 1933, pp. 20 ff. ('Zehn-jahr-Annalen'). The English version quoted above is taken from Gurney, op. cit., p. 174.

from the time when I sat down on my father's throne I conquered those hostile countries and destroyed them.

Similar passages occur again and again in these annals.[71] Further expressions of the same belief are found in the prayers of the same Hittite king, Mursilis II. In one of the well-known so-called Plague Prayers[72] the Storm-god is directly described as the true agent:

When the Hattian Storm-god had brought people of Kurustama to the country of Egypt . . .'[73]

Though the context is of course different, this passage recalls the famous words in the Book of Amos (9.7), which are usually interpreted as evidence for the belief that 'Yahweh is Lord of the whole of human history':[74]

הלוא את־ישראל העליתי מארץ	Did I not bring up Israel from
מצרים ופלשתיים מכפתור וארם	the land of Egypt, and the Phili-
מקיר:	stines from Caphtor and the Sy-
	rians from Kir?

In another prayer the king complains about rebellious neighbours:[75]

. . . now these lands also have set themselves free from the Sun-goddess of Arinna and have cast off (their) tribute (like a burden), and are beginning in their turn to attack the land of Hatti. For of old the land of Hatti with the help of the Sun-goddess of Arinna used to rage(?) against the surrounding lands like a lion. . . . But now all the surrounding countries have begun to attack the land of Hatti. And unto the Sun-goddess of Arinna let it become again (an occasion for) vengeance; and, O deity, bring not thy name into contempt.

---

[71] E.g. Obv. II: 3 ff.: '. . . Und die Sonnengöttin von Arinna, meine Herrin, der stolze Wettergott, mein Herr, Mezzullaš und die Götter alle standen mir bei, da schlug ich den Pišhurischen Feind . . .' (Goetze, op. cit., p. 45); cf. II: 25 f. (p. 51); II: 38 f. (pp. 55 ff.); II: 61 f. (p. 63); Rev. III: 28 f. (p. 75); III: 41 f. (pp. 77 ff.), etc. On the term for the divine power manifested in victories, parā hand(and)ātar, see further below, p. 111, n. 42.

[72] Published by Goetze, 'Die Pestgebete des Muršiliš', Kleinasiatische Forschungen, hrsg. von F. Sommer und H. Ehelolf, 1, Weimar 1930, pp. 161 ff.

[73] Op. cit., p. 208 f. The English version quoted above is Goetze's own in ANET², p. 395.

[74] H. E. W. Fosbroke, 'The Book of Amos. Introduction and Exegesis', IB 6, New York–Nashville 1956, p. 848; cf. also p. 769.

[75] Gurney, 'Hittite Prayers of Mursili II', AAA 27, 1940, p. 31 (C II, ll. 41 ff.).

The political and military situation is clearly the concern of the goddess. A similar divine solicitude for the social order of the country is implied in a hymn to the Sun-god:[76]

> O Sun-God, my lord! Just lord of judgment! O king of heaven and earth! Thou rulest the lands. ... Thou establishest custom and contract of the land, O Sun-God, mighty king!

The same divine concern for the realm of history, the same power to govern the course of events is presupposed in several passages in the Amarna letters. Tushratta, king of Mitanni, writes to Amenophis III (tablet 19, l. 14):[77]

ilāni li-me-eš-še-ru-šu-nu-ti-ma	May the gods govern so that we
ša ni-ir-ta-'a-a-mu an-ni-[ka]	remain friends [like this]!
ᵈtešub (IM) be-e-li ù ᵈa-ma-nu-um	Teshub, my lord, and Amon may
a-na da-ra-a-ti ki-i ša i-na-a[n-na]	forever ordain it as it is no[w]!
lu-ú li-ni-ib-bi[-ú].	

Of course, this idea of historical events as governed by divine power dominates large sections of the Old Testament. Yhwh is Lord of history; he controls not only the destinies of nations:

משגיא לגוים ויאבדם	He makes nations great, and destroys them,
שטח לגוים וינחם:	he enlarges nations, and leads them away.
	(Job 12.23)

but also the minor incidents in the history of a particular people:

ויהוה צוה להפר את־עצת	For Yhwh had ordained to defeat
אחיתפל הטובה לבעבור הביא	the good counsel of Ahithophel,
יהוה אל־אבשלום את־הרעה:	so that Yhwh might bring evil upon Absalom. (2 Sam. 17.14)

This is characteristic of the Israelite view of history. But the quotations from extra-biblical sources have shown that it is also a conviction which the Israelites shared with other peoples in the ancient Near East.

---

[76] Quoted in an article by H. G. Güterbock, 'The Vocative in Hittite', *JAOS* 65, 1945, p. 251 ('the great Sun hymn XXXI 127').

[77] Knudtzon, op. cit., pp. 136 f. Similarly the idea that the historical relations between Egypt and the Hittite kingdom are jointly effected by the Egyptian and the Hittite gods is expressed in a passage in the treaty between Hattusilis III and Ramses II: see Weidner, *Politische Dokumente aus Kleinasien*, p. 114, ll. 11 ff.; English translation by Goetze in *ANET²*, p. 202. Cf. also Gurney, *The Hittites*, p. 140.

CHAPTER THREE

Kingship and Divine Rule in History

In a report of the campaigns during his first year, found in the so-called Monolith Inscription, Shalmaneser III (858–824 B.C.) says *inter alia* (col. I, ll. 49 ff.):[1]

ina u₄-me-šú-ma ad-lu-ul nar-bu-ut	At that time, I paid homage to the
ilāni[meš] *rabūti*[meš] *šá* [d]*aš+šur ù*	greatness of the great gods (and)
[d]*šá-maš qur-di-šú-nu ú-šá-pa ana*	extolled for posterity the heroic
ṣa-a-te ṣa-lam šarrū-ti-ia šur-ba-a	achievements of Ashur and
ēpuš[uš] *il-ka-kat qur-di-ia ep-šet*	Shamash and fashioned a
taš-nin-ti-ia ina qé-reb-šú al-ṭur	magnificent stele with myself
	as king. I wrote my heroic acts
	and valorous deeds on it.[1a]

Again historical events are obviously regarded as divine actions. But the wording is noteworthy: Shalmaneser extols the heroic achievements of the gods by recording *his own* deeds. The military successes of the king are in reality the gods'. This leads us to the question of the king as the instrument through which the deity acts in history.

The royal inscriptions of Sumer and Akkad sometimes seem rather bombastic, and they have been interpreted as arrogant boasting. Their purpose is supposed to have been to glorify the ruler's own exploits.[2]

---

[1] F. E. Peiser, 'Die Monolith-Inschrift III Rawl. 7—8', *Keilinschriftliche Bibliothek*, ed. E. Schrader, I, Berlin 1889, pp. 158 f. English translations of this passage are found, e.g., in Luckenbill, *Ancient Records of Assyria and Babylonia*, I, p. 215, and in *ANET*², p. 277 (translator: Oppenheim).

[1a] Cf. *CAD* s. v. *alaktu*.

[2] See e.g. Mowinckel, 'Die vorderasiatischen Königs- und Fürsteninschriften. Eine stilistische Studie', *EYXAPIΣTHPION. Studien zur Religion und Literatur des Alten und Neuen Testaments Hermann Gunkel . . . dargebracht . . .* (FRLANT N. F. 19), 1, Göttingen 1923, p. 282: 'Da es nun aber der Zweck der Inschriften war, den König möglichst zu verherrlichen und seine Verdienste als die grösste möglichen darzustellen, so war immer das Streben darauf gerichtet, eine möglichst ausführliche und erschöpfende Aufzählung aller seiner Grosstaten zu geben' (cf. also pp. 297 ff., the section 'Die Ichform und die Egozentrizität'); or Noth, 'Geschichtsschreibung I. Im AT', *RGG*³, II, col. 1499: '. . . die zahlreichen altorientalischen Königsinschriften, die zum Ruhm des jeweiligen Herrschers . . . die siegreichen Feldzüge aufzählen oder seine Bauten aufführen.'

But there is much to indicate that this interpretation, which may seem self-evident at a cursory glance, does not in fact contain the whole truth. It is necessary to keep in mind that the long and detailed descriptions of the deeds of the ruler do not, despite their quantitative predominance, occupy the key position in the royal inscriptions. Properly they are an introduction to the main point in the inscriptions, which is the dedication of an object or, most frequently, a building to the gods by the king. The growth of Assyrian historiography has been well epitomized by A. T. E. Olmstead: it 'developed from the building inscription and not from the boast of the soldier'.[3] The later type of Assyrian and Babylonian royal inscriptions 'represents an ingenious adaptation of an earlier prototype that, fundamentally, had the form of a votive inscription'.[4] This means that the texts reporting the royal victories and achievements are primarily to be seen as communications from the king to his god. They are not primarily intended to diffuse the rulers' fame far and wide: in fact the 'longest and most explicit Assyrian royal inscriptions discovered to date were imbedded in the substructure of a temple or a palace, safe from human eyes and only to be read by the deity to which they were addressed.'[5] And in a text where the king does expect his inscription to be read by men and states this explicitly, he does not boast of his exploits and take the credit to himself but records them *ad maiorem dei gloriam*: Nebuchadnezzar II says in a building inscription dealing with the restoration of Eulla, the temple of Ninkarrak in Sippar (col. III, ll. 3 ff.):[6]

---

[3] *Assyrian Historiography. A Source Study* (The University of Missouri Studies. Social Science Series, III: 1), Columbia, Missouri, 1916, p. 64.

[4] A. L. Oppenheim, *Ancient Mesopotamia. Portrait of a Dead Civilization*, Chicago–London 1964, p. 26. Cf. also pp. 146 ff., and Mowinckel, op. cit., pp. 313 ff.

[5] Oppenheim, op. cit., p. 147. This is true of a great many inscriptions: 'All cylinders, prisms, cones, and brick inscriptions were hidden in walls and foundation boxes.' (p. 148). From the fact that the information in openly displayed stelae is of the same type as that in buried cylinders Oppenheim concludes that the former category was not intended for the information of the beholder either (ibid.). Cf. also Mowinckel, op. cit., pp. 311 ff., and J. Læssøe, *People of Ancient Assyria. Their Inscriptions and Correspondence*, London 1963, pp. 160 f.

[6] Langdon–Zehnpfund, op. cit., p. 110. The inscription ('Nebukadnezar Nr. 13') is described on pp. 21 ff., and its text is found on pp. 102 ff. Oddly enough Mowinckel quotes this particular passage in support of the view 'dass die Inschriften... das Verdienst des Urhebers vor den Göttern hervorheben wollen' (op. cit., p. 312 f.). There are certainly some passages on which such a claim could be based, but I cannot find that Nebuchadnezzar here speaks of his own merits before the gods: on the contrary he gives the credit to them. The same formulation is found in another inscription, 'Nebukadnezar Nr. 1', Col. II, ll. 49 ff. (Langdon–Zehnpfund, p. 76).

ka-le-e ep-še-e-ti-ia ša i-na narî	All my deeds, which I have
aš-ṭu-ru mu-da-a li-ta-am-ma-	written on the stele, the wise
ar-ma ta-ni-it-ti ilâni li-iḫ-ta-as-	shall read and shall remember
sa-as	the praise of the gods.[7]

The king's achievements give cause for the praise of the gods because he has not acted on his own behalf but as their representative and instrument. And it is precisely in their capacity as the representatives of the gods on earth, who have to render account to the real king, that the Oriental rulers speak in their inscriptions.[8] Their reports of the military campaigns are not analogous to Caesar's *De Bello Gallico* but to his official reports to the senate at their pre-literary stage.[9] E. A. Speiser has supplemented this argument by establishing a link between the annals and the *Gattung* called letters to the gods.[10] The enumeration of the glorious deeds, then, is not so much self-praise as an account of how the god's commission had been executed: 'the missions recorded were the god's missions'.[11] The big words were justified because ulti-

---

[7] In view of such passages one is tempted to suggest that the inaccessibility of the inscriptions is perhaps slightly overemphasized by Oppenheim, though it is of course an important aspect. Perhaps it could be argued that a development has taken place so that the later inscriptions exhibit a growing tendency among the kings to write for human eyes: cf. R. Laqueur, 'Formen geschichtlichen Denkens im alten Orient und Okzident', *NJWJ* 7, 1931, p. 500.—In this connexion the Behistun inscription of Darius is of interest, as Prof. J. Aro points out to me. It was carved on an inaccessible rock and certainly could not be read by the passers-by. However, Darius seems to have taken effective measures in order to promulgate the contents of the inscription: it was widely distributed in Aramaic, as can be seen from the archive at Elephantine. Since much of the Achaemenid administrative procedure was borrowed from the Assyrians and the Neo-Babylonian Empire, one could conjecture that royal inscriptions were already earlier translated into Aramaic and sent e.g. to the various provinces of the Assyrian Empire. It appears that though these inscriptions were formally addressed to the deity, their contents were meant to be known by the subjects too.

[8] This has been emphasized by Laqueur, op. cit., p. 493.

[9] This parallel has been drawn by E. Täubler, 'Die Anfänge der Geschichtschreibung', *Tyche. Historische Studien*, Leipzig–Berlin 1926, p. 42, and also by Laqueur, op. cit., p. 493 (apparently independently of Täubler: there is no reference to *Tyche*).

[10] E. A. Speiser, 'Ancient Mesopotamia', *The Idea of History in the Ancient Near East*, ed. R. C. Dentan (AOS 38), New Haven 1955, pp. 65 ff. A similar point is made by A. Moortgat in A. Scharff–A. Moortgat, *Ägypten und Vorderasien im Altertum*, München 1950, p. 429. Cf. already A. Ungnad, 'Der Gottesbrief als Form assyrischer Kriegsberichterstattung', *OLZ* 21, 1918, col. 72 ff. (which Speiser and Moortgat do not mention).

[11] Speiser, op. cit., p. 66. Cf. C. J. Gadd, *Ideas of Divine Rule in the Ancient East* (The Schweich Lectures of the British Academy 1945), London 1948, p. 62: 'The wars were the god's wars, the king his general'. This is also stressed by H. Gese in

mately the inscriptions served the purpose of glorifying the god, not his representative. On this interpretation the annals are evidence for the concept of history as divine deeds not only in individual passages or expressions but by their very existence and purpose: they are based on the idea that the deity is the real lord of history and that the achievements testify to his power.

Obviously the Mesopotamian royal ideology is relevant in this connexion. According to Assyrian and Babylonian ideas the king is the god's representative.[12] This is evident from early Sumerian times and down through the centuries. In his paper on Sumerian historiography, Kramer points out that the secular ruler of the city of Lagash in the early third millennium B.C. 'ruled the city as the representative of the tutelary deity',[13] who was held to be the real sovereign. The king's capacity as a deputy of the god is clearly expressed in some of the royal titles in Mesopotamian inscriptions, particularly *šakkanakku* (GÌR.NITA)[14] and *šaknu*,[15] both meaning approximately 'deputy, vicegerent, governor'.

GÌR.NITA = *šakkanakku* was not always a royal title: in the Ur III period, i.e. the last century of the third millennium B.C., it was bestowed on subordinate officials, dependent on the king of Ur.[16] In the Old Babylonian period it became a title of kings who were independent rulers; the background of this development is, of course, the idea of the tutelary deity as the true king and the human ruler as his 'viceroy'.[17] This epithet in the royal titulary thus expresses a subordinate status. It is used also by Assyrian kings of a later age: both Shalmaneser III (858–824 B.C.) and Assurbanipal (668–627 B.C.) once each bear the title *šakkanak* *daššur* 'viceroy of (the god) Ashur' in their inscriptions.[18]

Usually the name of the deity is thus mentioned in the title, but it may also be said more generally that the king is the deputy of the gods, as in the historical introduction in the inscriptions of Adad-nirari I,

---

his admirable article 'Geschichtliches Denken im Alten Orient und im Alten Testament', *ZThK* 55, 1958, pp. 137 f.

[12] See e.g. R. Labat, *Le caractère religieux de la royauté assyro-babylonienne* (Études d'assyriologie 2), Paris 1939, pp. 219 ff. (the section 'Le roi représentant des dieux sur la terre').

[13] *IEJ* 3, 1953, p. 227.

[14] See W. W. Hallo, *Early Mesopotamian Royal Titles: A Philologic and Historical Analysis* (AOS 43), New Haven 1957, pp. 100 ff.

[15] See O. Schroeder, 'Ueber *šaknu* in der assyrischen Königstitulatur', *OLZ* 20, 1917, col. 174 ff.

[16] Hallo, op. cit., p. 102.

[17] 'Viceroy' is Hallo's rendering of GÌR.NITA = *šakkanakku*: op. cit., p. 127.

[18] K. Tallqvist, *Der assyrische Gott* (StOr 4: 3), Helsingforsiae 1932, p. 12.

who calls himself *ša-ka-an-ki ilâni*[meš] 'the viceroy of the gods'.[19] And the term is also employed in a less formal way: at the end of a very long inscription commemorating *inter alia* the conquest of Lebanon and a victory over the Egyptian army, engraved in identical wording on both sides of the pass of Wadi Brisa, a narrow valley in Mount Lebanon, Nebuchadnezzar II says to his god Marduk (col. X, ll. 33 f.):[20]

a-na-ku lu-ú šakkanakka-ka	I am indeed your faithful
ki-i-nim lu-uš-du-ud	*šakkanakku*; may I bear your
si-ir-da-a-ka	yoke.

A title commonly applied to the Assyrian kings is *šakin* [d]*enlil* 'vice-gerent of Enlil'. It occurs in many inscriptions from different ages. Shamshi-Adad I (1813–1781 B.C.) in the opening lines of a clay tablet styles himself:[21]

[d]*šamši*[ši]-[d]*adad šar kiššati ša-ki-in*	Shamshi-Adad, king of the
[d]*en-líl*	universe, vicegerent of Enlil ...

Shalmaneser I (1274–1245 B.C.) uses this title both of himself, of his father Adad-nirari I (1307–1275 B.C.) and of his grandfather Arik-den-ili (1319–1308 B.C.) in a building inscription of which a great many copies have been preserved:[22]

[Id]*šùl-ma-nu-ašarēdu šakni* [d]*enlil*	Shalmaneser, vicegerent of Enlil,
iššak (SANGA) *aš-šur apil adad-*	governor of Ashur,[23] son of Adad-
narâri šakni [d]*enlil iššak aš-šur apil*	nirari, vicegerent of Enlil, governor
arik-dên-ili ša-ak-ni [d]*enlil iššak*	of Ashur, son of Arik-den-ili,
[d]*aš-šur-ma*	vicegerent of Enlil, governor
	of Ashur ...

These formulations recur also in other inscriptions by Shalmaneser,[24]

---

[19] Ebeling–Meissner–Weidner, *Die Inschriften der altassyrischen Könige*, p. 56, text no. 1, l. 2. The text is described on pp. XXII ff. Weidner takes *ša-ka-an-ki* to be 'schlechte Schreibung für *šakkanakki*' (p. 56, n. 4).

[20] Langdon–Zehnpfund, *Die neubabylonischen Königsinschriften*, p. 176. A description of the text 'Nebukadnezar Nr. 19' is found on pp. 33 ff., a transliteration and a German translation on pp. 150 ff.

[21] Ebeling–Meissner–Weidner, op. cit., p. 26, text no. 5.

[22] Op. cit., pp. XXXII ff. (list of duplicates); 126 (text).

[23] Cf. Hallo, op. cit., pp. 34 ff. Weidner translates 'der Priester Aššurs' (Ebeling—Meissner–Weidner, op. cit., p. 127).

[24] See e.g. Ebeling–Meissner–Weidner, op. cit., pp. 130, 140 (text no. 8), 152 (text no. 14) etc.

and are repeated by his son and successor Tukulti-Ninurta I (1244–1208 B.C.); e.g. in an inscription written on small tablets of gold and silver:[25]

[túkul-ti-^{d}nin-urta šakni ^{d}enlil iššak (SANGA) ^{d}aš-šur	Tukulti-Ninurta, vicegerent of Enlil, governor of Ashur . . .

A late example is found in a long building inscription by Esarhaddon (680–669 B.C.); the introductory lines run:[26]

[aššur]-ahu-iddina^{na} šarru rabû^ú šarru dan-nu šar kiš-šá-ti šar mât aš-šur^{ki} šá-ak-nu ^{d}en-líl	[Esar]haddon, the great king, the mighty king, king of the universe, king of Assyria, vicegerent of Enlil . . .

These titles, borne for centuries by Assyrian kings, testify to the belief that the king is the deputy of the god on earth, he is a king *dei gratia*, executing divine decisions, an instrument in the hand of the real ruler. 'Die *šaknu*-Titulatur der assyrischen Könige ist somit ein Ausdruck demütiger Unterordnung unter die göttliche Gewalt.'[27]

There is of course evidence for this idea other than the royal titles. Numerous inscriptions emphasize that the king is commissioned to act on behalf of the god. In a Sumerian text which seems to derive from the time of the first dynasty of Isin[28] (i.e. the beginning of the second millennium B.C.), Enlil, the ruler of the land, commissions Utuhegal, the king of Uruk, to defeat the Gutians and to reestablish the dominion of Uruk over Sumer:[29]

> Gutium [which had committed acts of violence, described in ll. 2–14] Enlil, le roi des contrées, de détruire (jusqu'à) son nom, à Utu-hegal, le mâle fort, le roi d'Uruk, le roi des quatre régions, le roi dont la parole est sans rivale, Enlil, le roi des contrées, donna mission.[30]

---

[25] Weidner, *Die Inschriften Tukulti-Ninurtas I.*, inscription no. 13, pp. IX f. (description), 22 (text), obv., ll. 1 f. The same phrase recurs in ll. 18 f. Cf. also p. 32, inscr. no. 19, ll. 3 f., and p. 36, inscr. no. 25, ll. 1 f.

[26] Borger, *Die Inschriften Asarhaddons*, p. 1, the inscription 'Ass. A.', col. I, ll. 1 ff. The title 'vicegerent of Enlil' occurs also in the inscription 'AsBbA', obv., l. 22, p. 80.

[27] Schroeder, op. cit., col. 176. Schroeder also calls attention to the fact 'dass auch die Bezeichnung christlicher Könige als Herrscher „Von Gottes Gnaden" (dei gratia) zunächst nicht in dem stolzen Sinn eines Selbstherrschers gemeint war, sondern dem *šaknu*-Titel gleich einen Verzicht an Würden darstellte.' (ibid.).

[28] F. Thureau-Dangin, 'La fin de la domination gutienne', *RA* 9, 1912, pp. 111 ff.

[29] Cf. P. T. Paffrath, *Zur Götterlehre in den altbabylonischen Königsinschriften* (Studien zur Geschichte und Kultur des Altertums 6: 5–6), Paderborn 1913, p. 219.

[30] Thureau-Dangin, op. cit., p. 114 (col. I, ll. 1 ff.).

Enlil acts in history through his deputy, the king.

Another Sumerian inscription[31] narrates how the deity—in this case Utu, the Sumerian counterpart of Shamash—selects Nur-Adad (who reigned 1865–1850 B.C.) to carry out his decision to recapture and restore the city of Larsa, which had been conquered by enemy forces:

> [Utu, le r]oi de L[arša?] ... à la suite de sa s[age] décision son cœur l'incita à restaurer la ville de sa seigneurerie. Il choisit un pasteur juste (et) le prit parmi les foules nombreuses: mon père qui m'a engendré, Nūradad. Il l'éleva à la royauté du pays de Sumer. Dans l'Ebabbar, le temple, vie de Sumer, il lui mit dans la main le sceptre qui courbe le pays hostile.[32]

Here again the deity is active in historical events, but he uses the king as a representative to carry out his plans.[33]

Examples can easily be multiplied. The same idea of a divine control of the course of events so to speak by proxy is expressed on a stele inscribed with a charter of the time of Nebuchadnezzar I (1124–1103 B.C.), which begins (col. I, ll. 1 ff.):[34]

e-nu-ma ^{d}*nabû-ku-dúr-ri-uṣur rubû na-a-du... ú-ta-'-ir-šu-ma šar ilâni*^{meš} ^{d}*marduk a-na tur-ri gi-mil-li* ^{kur}*akkadi*^{ki} *ú-šat-ba-a kakkê*^{meš}*-šu*	When Nebuchadnezzar, the pious prince, ... (there follows a series of epithets, ll. 2–11)–when the king of the gods, Marduk, sent him forth, he raised his weapons to avenge Akkad.

A stone tablet recording Nabu-apla-iddina's (9th century B.C.) re-endowment of the sun-temple at Sippar speaks of the king's tasks which the deity has given him to execute (col. II, ll. 18 f.; 29 ff.–III.10):[35]

^{d}*nabú-aplu-iddina*^{na} *šar bâbili*^{ki} ... *šá ana tu-ur gi-mil* ^{kur}*akkadi*^{ki} *šu-šub ma-ḫa-zi na-de-e parakkê*^{meš} *uṣ-ṣur uṣurâti*^{meš} *šul-lum parṣê*^{meš} *u pil-lu-de-e kun-ni sat-tuk-ki šur-ru-uḫ*	Nabu-apla-iddina, the king of Babylon, ... to whom the great lord Marduk entrusted the righteous sceptre, the shepherding of the peoples, to avenge Akkad, to make cities habitable, to found

---

[31] J. van Dijk, 'Une insurrection générale au pays de Larša avant l'avènement de Nūradad', JCS 19, 1965, pp. 1 ff.

[32] Op. cit., p. 7, ll. 91 ff.

[33] Cf. Labat, op. cit., p. 35: 'Le véritable souverain de la ville est donc bien le dieu. Le prince qu'il choisit parmi les hommes est le dépositaire de sa puissance et l'exécuteur de ses volontés.'

[34] King, *Babylonian Boundary-Stones*, p. 31.

[35] King, op. cit., p. 122 f.

nindabê^{meš} *bêlu rabû*^u ^d*marduk*	sanctuaries, to prepare reliefs,
ḫatta i-šar-ta re-'-ut niše^{meš} *e-pe-ši*	to put in order rites and cult
ú-mal-lu-ú qa-tuš-šú	objects, to establish regular
	sacrifices, to increase offerings.[36]

Through the chosen instrument, the king, the deity's purposes are carried out both in the political and social, and in the cultic domains. And because the king is thus nothing but a representative of the divine ruler, rebellion is not simply described as an act of disobedience towards a human master but is regarded as insubordination against the god himself. This is evident *inter alia* from a passage in the inscription of Esarhaddon (680–669 B.C.) which tells about the desertion of a Sidonian king:[37]

^I*ab-di-mil-ku-ut-ti šàr* ^{uru}*si-dun-ni*	Abdi-Milkutti, the king of Sidon,
la pa-liḫ be-lu-ti-ia la še-mu-u	who did not fear my lordship and
zi-kir šap-ti-ia ša eli tam-tim	did not obey the word of my lips
gal-la-tim it-tak-lu-ma is-lu-u	but trusted the rolling sea and
^{giš}*nir* ^d*aš-šur*	threw off the yoke of (the god)
	Ashur, . . .

To rebel against the Assyrian king is to throw off the yoke of the Assyrian god. The power and dominion which the king exercises is the god's. This is constantly apparent from the royal inscriptions, *inter alia* from a characteristic formulation by Nebuchadnezzar II, who says that Nebo, the son of Marduk, had committed his reign to the king's charge: *ip-qi-du ba-ú-la-a-tu-šu* 'he entrusted (me) with his subjects'.[38]

One of the most striking expressions of this idea of divine historical deeds executed through the king is found in Assyrian art. In the famous reliefs of Ashurnasirpal there is a complete conformity between the god's movements and activities and those of the king. When Ashurnasirpal draws his bow in combat, the god Ashur too, suspended in the air above the king in a winged solar disc, is pictured with his bow drawn, and when after the battle the king lets his bow drop, Ashur holds his in exactly the same position.[39] The identity of the divine and the royal deed is patent.

---

[36] Cf. the translation of this passage by W. G. Lambert, *AfO* 18, 1957–58, p. 398.

[37] Borger, op. cit., p. 48 (the inscription 'Nin. A—F', episode no. 5, A, II: 65 ff.).

[38] Langdon–Zehnpfund, op. cit., p. 134: 'Nebukadnezar Nr. 15', Col. VII, l. 29.–Cf. also the numerous references to the royal insignia as symbols of the divine power: Labat, op. cit., pp. 89 ff.

[39] E. A. W. Budge, *Assyrian Sculptures in the British Museum. Reign of Ashur-nasirpal, 885—860 B.C.*, London 1914, Plates XIV, 1 and XVII, 1. Cf. also the interpretation of these reliefs in Labat, op. cit., pp. 261 ff. and in the essay on Sumerian

It seems reasonable to conclude that the royal ideology in Mesopotamia must have facilitated the idea of historical events as divine manifestations. Of course it is not a sufficient explanation of this conception: obviously many other actions than those of the king were held to be divine deeds, but it may justly be regarded as one aspect of it.

Naturally this idea of kingship as a divine rule was not restricted to Mesopotamia but common to the entire ancient Near East. In the Hittite texts, there are some unmistakable allusions to the divine appointment of the ruler.[40] These are the words spoken by a priest during a cultic act performed by the king:

> May *Tabarnas*, the king, be pleasing to the gods. The land belongs to the weather-god. Heaven and earth with the people belong to the weather-god, and he has made the *labarnas* [*sic*], the king, his administrator and has given him the whole land of Hattusas. Labarnas shall administer the whole land with his hands.[41]

A ritual for the building of a new palace also represents the king as the steward of the gods:

> To me, the king, have the gods, the sun-god and the weather-god, entrusted the land and my house.[42]

And in a treaty between the Hittite king Suppiluliumas (c. 1380–1340 B.C.) and the king of Mitanni, written in Akkadian, the following passage is found (rev., l. 35):[43]

me-ḫi-ir tup-pi an-ni-ti a-na pa-ni	A duplicate of this tablet is laid
^{d}*šamaš* ^{uru}*a-ri-i[n-n]a ša-kin*^{in}	down before the sun(-goddess)
ki-me-e ^{d}*šamaš* ^{uru}*a-ri-in-na*	of Arinna, as the sun(-goddess)
šarru-ut-ta ù ^{sal}*šarrat-ut-ta*	of Arinna ordains kingship and
ú-ma-'-ar	queenship.

and Babylonian-Assyrian religion by O. E. Ravn in *Illustreret Religionshistorie*, ed. J. Pedersen, København 1948, p. 150. It is generally agreed that the god with the bow is Ashur, but B. Pering has maintained that he is Ninurta: 'Die geflügelte Scheibe in Assyrien. Eine religionsgeschichtliche Untersuchung', *AfO* 8, 1932—33, pp. 281 ff., especially p. 295, and Tallqvist suggests Shamash: *Der assyrische Gott*, pp. 106 f.

[40] Gurney, 'Hittite Kingship', *Myth, Ritual, and Kingship. Essays on the Theory and Practice of Kingship in the Ancient Near East and in Israel*, ed. S. H. Hooke, Oxford 1958, p. 113.

[41] Op. cit., pp. 113 f.

[42] Op. cit., p. 114.

[43] Weidner, *Politische Dokumente aus Kleinasien*, p. 26 ('Vertrag zwischen Šubbiluliuma, König von Hatti, und Mattiuaza, König von Mitanni'). Cf. also Gurney, op. cit., p. 109.

Among the Hittites too the kings were held to act on behalf of the gods, who were the real rulers.

As is well known, similar ideas were associated also with the Israelite king. Yhwh, the lord of the whole earth, delegates his dominion to his son, the king,[44] who is his representative on earth; 'the king held office as Yahweh's agent or vicegerent'.[45] The king is not only the representative of the people before Yhwh but also Yhwh's representative before the people; Yhwh commissions his anointed to act on his behalf and to execute his purposes. Thus there is to a certain extent an identification of royal actions with divine.[46] This must not, however, be taken to imply that the Israelite conception of kingship played any important role in the formation of the Old Testament idea of historical events as divine actions. In the first place, there is hardly such a thing as *the* Hebrew view of kingship: rather we must reckon with different attitudes in different circles of Hebrew society;[47] this is

---

[44] E.g. 2 Sam. 7.14; Ps. 2; 18.44 f.; 72.8 ff.; 144.2; 1 Chr. 17.13. Cf. K.-H. Bernhardt, *Das Problem der altorientalischen Königsideologie im Alten Testament unter besonderer Berücksichtigung der Geschichte der Psalmenexegese dargestellt und kritisch gewürdigt* (SupplVT 8), Leiden 1961, pp. 86 f.; 262.

[45] A. R. Johnson, 'Hebrew Conceptions of Kingship', *Myth, Ritual, and Kingship*, p. 207.

[46] This identification is also expressed in the famous and much disputed passage in Ps. 45.7. The king is called אלהים 'divine being': כסאך אלהים עולם ועד 'Your throne, O god, is for ever and ever'. Many commentators have tried to avoid this straight-forward translation. One method of explaining away the plain meaning of the passage is to translate 'Your throne is like that of God' with reference to Cant. 1.15; 4.1 עיניך יונים 'your eyes are doves' which is then supposed to mean 'your eyes are like those of doves' (so C. R. North, 'The Religious Aspects of Hebrew Kingship', *ZAW* 50, 1932, pp. 29 f.; J. de Fraine, *L'aspect religieux de la royauté israélite* (Analecta Biblica 3), Roma 1954, p. 269, n. 6; A. R. Johnson, *Sacral Kingship in Ancient Israel*, Cardiff 1955, p. 27, n. 1). It should be noted that the two passages in Cant. cannot any longer reasonably be invoked in support of this translation, since G. Gerleman has shown that עיניך יונים means simply 'your eyes are doves', *not* 'your eyes are like those of doves'—the comparison is not with the eyes of the birds but with the contours of their bodies. In the conventional art of the ancients, especially that of the ancient Egyptians, certain details had a stereotyped form. 'Zu diesen konventionell gestalteten Einzelheiten gehört das Auge, das durchgehend in einer Form konturiert ist, die an einen Vogelkörper sehr stark erinnert.' (G. Gerleman, *Ruth. Das Hohelied* (BKAT 18), Neukirchen-Vluyn 1965, p. 114; cf. also pp. 146 f.). This convincing interpretation of the passages in Cant. finally disposes of the alleged support for the mitigatory translation of Ps. 45.7. Cf. also J. R. Porter, 'Psalm XLV.7', *JTS* N.S. 12, 1961, pp. 51 ff.

[47] This seems to have been strangely disregarded in the sometimes rather heated scholarly controversies about the sacral kingship in Israel but is rightly emphasized by H. Ringgren, *Israelitische Religion* (Die Religionen der Menschheit 26), Stuttgart

evident already from the divergent views of the origin of Israelite monarchy which appear in the Books of Samuel. Secondly—and this is no doubt important—the monarchy is a comparatively late institution in Israel,[48] so that all the characteristic traits of the Hebrew belief in Yhwh's acts on the plane of history were developed 'before there reigned any king over the children of Israel'. The situation was different in Mesopotamia: there the monarchy was age-old, it was thought to belong to the primeval structure of society—according to the Sumerian King List 'kingship was lowered from heaven'[49] in the very beginning, long before the Flood—and so the ideas of the king as the gods' agent could there become one factor—albeit not a vital one—in the belief in a divine activity in history.

1963, pp. 201 ff. Cf. also the significant plural form in the title of A. R. Johnson's essay quoted above: 'Hebrew Conceptions of Kingship'.

[48] This is strongly emphasized by Noth in his discussion of the sacral kingship in Israel: 'Die auffälligste geschichtliche Tatsache im Blick auf das Königtum in Israel ist die, dass Israel erst spät dazu gekommen ist, diese Einrichtung zu schaffen.' ('Gott, König, Volk im Alten Testament. Eine methodologische Auseinandersetzung mit einer gegenwärtigen Forschungsrichtung', *ZThK* 47, 1950, p. 174= *Gesammelte Studien zum Alten Testament* (ThB 6), München 1957, p. 209). The conclusion that Noth draws from this fact is however not necessarily valid (p. 178=213): because the Israelites knew their monarchy to be a late institution, they could not, according to Noth, believe in kingship as an 'Element einer zeitlos gültigen göttlichen Weltordnung'. This is certainly to overrate the influence of historical knowledge on religious beliefs in the ancient Near East: Ashurnasirpal II claims to be 'born amid unknown mountains' although *in the same text* he states that he is the son of a king of Assyria! (see H. Winckler, *Altorientalische Geschichts-Auffassung* (Ex Oriente Lux II: 2), Leipzig 1906, pp. 47 f.).

[49] *ANET*², p. 265 (translator: Oppenheim).

CHAPTER FOUR

The Divine Word and the Course of Events

The power of the divine word is a common theme in ancient Oriental hymns and prayers, as it is in the Old Testament. The following lines from a Sumerian hymn to Nanna the moon-god provide a characteristic example of the rich and varied expressions for the overwhelming power of the word of the god:

> Thou! When thy word is pronounced in heaven the Igigi prostrate themselves.
> Thou! When thy word is pronounced on earth the Anunnaki kiss the ground.
> Thou! When thy word drifts along in heaven like the wind it makes rich the feeding and drinking of the land.
> Thou! When thy word settles down on the earth green vegetation is produced.
> Thou! Thy word makes fat the sheepfold and the stall; it makes living creatures widespread.
> Thou! Thy word causes truth and justice to be, so that the people speak the truth.
> Thou! Thy word which is far away in heaven, which is hidden in the earth is something no one sees.
> Thou! Who can comprehend thy word, who can equal it?[1]

---

[1] *ANET²*, p. 386 (translator: F. J. Stephens). The latest translation is by Å. Sjöberg, *Der Mondgott Nanna-Suen in der sumerischen Überlieferung. I. Teil: Texte*, Stockholm 1960, pp. 165 ff. (the passage quoted above is found on p. 166). The text derives from a time shortly after the Old Babylonian period: see Sjöberg, op. cit., p. 171. Cf. also Falkenstein's translation in Falkenstein–von Soden, *Sumerische und Akkadische Hymnen und Gebete*, pp. 222 ff. For other ancient Near Eastern texts describing the divine word and its effects see J. Szeruda, *Das Wort Jahwes. Eine Untersuchung zur israelitisch-jüdischen Religionsgeschichte*, Łódź 1921, p. 38 ff.; O. Grether, *Name und Wort Gottes im Alten Testament* (BZAW 64), Giessen 1934, pp. 139 ff.; and above all L. Dürr, *Die Wertung des göttlichen Wortes im Alten Testament und im antiken Orient. Zugleich ein Beitrag zur Vorgeschichte des neutestamentlichen Logosbegriffes* (MVAG 42: 1), Leipzig 1938, pp. 2 ff. (the section entitled 'Die „Macht des göttlichen Wortes" in altorientalischen Hymnen und Gebeten...'). Cf. also M. Jastrow, *Die Religion Babyloniens und Assyriens*, I,

The divine word is conceived as a 'physisch-kosmische Potenz',[2] a cosmic power that has created the world and now maintains it, that bestows life and renews it.[3] Thus it is above all in the world of nature that the effects of the divine word are traced.

On the basis of this observation a rather sharp distinction has been made: it is often said to be something peculiarly Israelite to regard the word of the deity as active not only in nature but also—and primarily—in history, while other Near Eastern religions are supposed to connect the divine word with creation and nature only, not with historical events. This has been maintained especially by Grether, who emphasized the alleged contrast rather categorically. On the one side: 'Jahwes dabar gilt als der Nerv der Geschichte, auf den die einzelnen Ereignisse durchgehends zurückgeführt werden';[4] on the other: 'Denn während diese Religionen [i.e. the religions of Israel's neighbours] das Wort als Prinzip der Geschichte nicht kennen und nicht kennen können, da sie das Geschehen nicht als Geschichte verstehen und keine Geschichtsbetrachtung üben, findet sich bei ihnen das Wort als wirksamer Faktor bei der Weltentstehung und im Naturgeschehen.'[5] According to this clear-cut division, the idea of the divine word as an 'active factor' in history is restricted to Israel and wholly unknown to other ancient Near Eastern peoples.

It is true that the extra-biblical texts quoted by Grether as also those adduced by Dürr favour this theory: they do in fact all of them speak almost exclusively of the power of the divine word in creation and nature.[6] But the selection is somewhat one-sided, and once we are allowed to go outside the rather narrow category of hymns describing and praising the word of the deity it is not difficult to adduce abundant

---

Giessen 1905, pp. 475 f.; II: 1, 1912, pp. 25 ff., 49 f., and B. Meissner, *Babylonien und Assyrien* II (Kulturgeschichtliche Bibliothek 1: 4), Heidelberg 1925, pp. 158 f., as well as Ringgren, *Word and Wisdom. Studies in the Hypostatization of Divine Qualities and Functions in the Ancient Near East,* Lund 1947, pp. 65 ff.

[2] Dürr, op. cit., p. 2. Szeruda, op. cit., p. 33, has 'kosmisch-physische Potenz'.

[3] Cf. the title of Dürr's second chapter: 'Das Wort Gottes als kosmische Kraft: Erschaffung und Erhaltung der Welt durch das göttliche Wort. Das Wort Gottes als Lebensvermittler und Lebensträger' (pp. 22 ff.).

[4] Grether, op. cit., p. 127 (primarily said of the Deuteronomic History).

[5] Op. cit., p. 139.

[6] Though already a passage in the hymn to Nanna quoted above (a text adduced also by Grether, p. 140) seems to indicate that 'Weltentstehung' and 'Naturgeschehen' are too narrow as descriptions of the field of action of the divine word: it 'causes truth and justice to be, so that the people speak the truth'— the world of justice and social relations cannot reasonably be brought in under the heading 'nature'.

evidence from Israel's environment for the idea of the divine word as effective in historical events as well. Grether's verdict cannot possibly be upheld; 'the word as an active factor in history' is clearly known also outside the Old Testament. The evidence is abundant and distributed over wide areas and different ages.

The divine word is mentioned in connexion with historical events in the Sumerian text recording the restoration of the boundary ditch between Lagash and Umma.[7] In one of the first sentences of the text we read:

> (Then) did Ningirsu, Enlil's foremost warrior, do battle with (the men of) Umma in accordance with his (Enlil's) straightforward word; by the word of Enlil he hurled the great Shush-net upon them, and heaped up their skeleton (?) piles in the plain in their (various) places.[8]

And further on in the same inscription it says:

> Entemena, the *ishakku* of Lagash, whose name was pronounced by Ningirsu, made this (boundary) ditch from the Tigris to the Idnun in accordance with the straightforward word of Enlil, in accordance with the straightforward word of Ningirsu, (and) in accordance with the straightforward word of Nanshe, (and) restored it for his beloved king Ningirsu and for his beloved queen Nanshe (after) he had constructed of bricks the foundation of the Namnunda-kigarra. May Shulutula, the (personal) god of Entemena, the *ishakku* of Lagash, whom Enlil gave the sceptre, whom Enki gave wisdom, whom Nanshe fixed upon (in her) heart, the great *ishakku* of Ningirsu, the man who had received the words of the gods, step forward (in prayer) for the life of Entemena before Ningirsu and Nanshe unto distant days.[9]

These passages not only testify to the concept of a divine control over the events of history but also show how this control is executed by means of the word of the gods, which is active in military and political affairs, determining the outcome of a battle and delimiting state frontiers.

A passage in the epilogue of the Code of Hammurapi (1792–1750 B.C.) expresses the same view of the divine word as an 'active factor in history'. In the curses directed against a future king who disregards

---

[7] Cf. above, pp. 17 f.; Kramer, 'Sumerian Historiography', *IEJ* 3, 1953, pp. 224 ff.
[8] Op. cit., p. 224.
[9] Op. cit., p. 226.

the ordinances prescribed by Hammurapi, the following formulation is found (rev. xxvi, ll. 73 ff.):[10]

ḫa-la-aq āli(URU)*-šu na-ás-pu-úḫ*	The destruction of his city, the
ni-ši-šu šar-ru-sú šu-pé-lam šum-šu	dispersion of his people, the
ù zi-kir-šu i-na ma-tim la šu-ub-	dethronement from his kingdom,
ša-a-am i-na pi(KA)*-šu kab-tim*	the disappearance of his name and
li-iq-bi	memory from the land may he
	(i.e. Enlil) order by his potent
	word!

It would seem that Grether's characterization of the Old Testament view of the relation between the divine word and the course of events, 'Der göttliche dabar setzt sich in geschichtliche Ereignisse um',[11] can also be used to describe the belief expressed by Hammurapi.

An Old Babylonian hymn to Ishtar, composed of fourteen stanzas of four lines each and containing at the end a prayer for Ammiditana (1683–1647 B.C.), the ninth king of the First Dynasty of Babylon, concludes with the following passage (ll. 49 ff.):[12]

si-iq-ru-uš-ša tu-ša-ak-ni-	By her word she has subjected
ša-aš-šu-um	to him
ki-ib-ra-at er-bé-e-em a-na	the four quarters (of the world)
še-pí-i-šu	to his feet,
ù na-ap-ḫa-ar ka-li-šu-nu	and the total of all dwelling-
da-ad-mi	places
ta-aṣ-ṣa-mi-su-nu-ti a-ni-	she has harnessed to his yoke.
ri-i-š(i)-ú	

The king's domination over his great empire is seen as the work of the goddess, and she has done this work through her word.

An almost identical formulation is found in a slightly earlier Old Babylonian text, a hymn to Nana for king Samsuiluna of Babylon

---

[10] The transliteration is taken from Borger's edition of Codex Hammurapi in his *Babylonisch-assyrische Lesestücke*, II, Roma 1963, p. 44. Cf. G. R. Driver—J. C. Miles, *The Babylonian Laws*, II, Oxford 1955, pp. 100 f. (transliteration and English translation). An English translation of the Code is also found in *ANET²*, pp. 163 ff. (translator: T. J. Meek).

[11] Op. cit., p. 127.

[12] Thureau–Dangin, 'Un hymne à Ištar de la haute époque babylonienne', *RA* 22, 1925, pp. 173 (transliteration), 177 (French translation). An English version of this hymn is found in *ANET²*, p. 383 (translator: F. J. Stephens), a German translation in Falkenstein–von Soden, *Sumerische und akkadische Hymnen und Gebete*, pp. 235 ff. (translator: von Soden).

(1749–1712 B.C.), whose rule is also regarded as the result of a divine command, (l. 53):[13]

qi-bi-tu-uš-ša mi-i[g-ru-u]š *e-te-el*	By her order her fav[ourite] is ruler.

A stele from the time of king Nebuchadnezzar I (1124–1103 B.C.) contains a passage where a certain event is described as having been put into execution through a divine word (ll. 40 f.):[14]

i-na pî ᵈ*iš-tar u* ᵈ*adad ilâni*ᵐᵉˢ *bêlê*ᵐᵉˢ *taḫâzi ul-te-es-ḫi-ir* *ḫul-te-lu-diš šar* ᵏᵘʳ*elamti*ᵏⁱ *i-te-mid šadâ-šú*	At the word of Ishtar and Adad, the gods who are lords of battle, he surrounded Hulteludish, king of Elam, and he disappeared for ever (lit., retreated to his moun- tain).

This mode of expression, that the king wrought his deeds 'at the word (order, command) of' a god or several gods is very frequent, especially in the royal inscriptions, in which it seems to be a standard formula remaining unaltered through the centuries. Several different words are used: *ina qibīt, ina siqir* (*zikir*), *ina pî, ina amāt*; they are on the whole synonymous. Thus Shalmaneser I (1274–1245 B.C.) sets out on a campaign at a divine order:[15]

*e-nu-ma i-na qí-bit ilâni*ᵐᵉˢ *rabûti*ᵐᵉˢ *i-na e-mu-qi ṣi-ra-ti šá* *aš-šur bêli-ia ana* ᵏᵘʳ*ḫa-ni-gal-bat* *alliku*ᵏᵘ*-ma*	When at the order of the great gods, in the exalted power of Ashur, my lord, I marched on Hanigalbat ...

and one of his successors, Ashur-resh-ishi I (1133–1116 B.C.), brings the surrounding countries under his control at the word of the war-god Ninurta, styling himself in an inscription:[16]

šá i-na siq-ri ᵈ*nin-urta qar-di* *ilâni*ᵐᵉˢ *e-liš u šap-liš* [... ...] *mâtât*ᵃᵗ [... ...] *lu-ul-lu-mi-i* *kúl-lat qu-ti-i ù na-gab ḫur-ša-*	...who at the word of Ninurta, the hero of the gods, above and below [... ...] the countries [... ...] of the Lullumî (and)

---

[13] von Soden, 'Altbabylonische Dialektdichtungen. 1. Ein Hymnus an Nanâ für Samsuiluna von Babylon (1913—1875)', *ZA* 44 (N.F. 10), 1938, pp. 34 (transliteration), 35 (German translation). See also the same author in Falkenstein–von Soden, op. cit., pp. 237 ff.; 381.

[14] King, *Babylonian Boundary-Stones*, p. 33.

[15] Ebeling–Meissner–Weidner, *Die Inschriften der altassyrischen Könige*, p. 116 (Salmanassar I, inscription no. 1, col. 2, ll. 16 ff.)

[16] Weidner, *Die Inschriften Tukulti-Ninurtas I.*, p. 54 (inscription no. 60, ll. 6 f.).

ni-šu-nu i-na-ru-ma a-na šêpê[II]-šú	of all the Qutî and overcame all
ú-šék-ni-šu	their highlands and subjected
	(them) under his feet.

Several centuries later Assurbanipal (668–627 B.C.) represents his supremacy as the work of the divine word; he describes himself as[17]

[rub]û la šá-na-an šá ina a-mat	[a prin]ce without equal, who at
[d]aššur [d][šamaš] [ù] [d]marduk ul-tu	the word of Ashur, [Shamash]
tam-tim e-lit a-di tam-tim šap-lit	[a]nd Marduk reigns from the
i-be-lu-ma [gi]-mir ma-lik	Upper Sea to the Lower Sea
ú-šak-niš še-pu-uš-[šú]	(and) has subjected [a]ll kings
	under [his] feet.

When the formula 'at the command of the god(s)' or 'at the word of the god(s)' occurs in these and similar connexions, describing royal conquests and military campaigns, it seems probable that the divine word referred to is some kind of oracle. Mesopotamian kings are known to have consulted diviners to ascertain the will of the gods before every important undertaking; the answer, obtained through different more or less elaborate uses of omens and regarded as a communication from the supernatural forces, would naturally be thought of as a 'word of the god'.[18] This is corroborated by a formulation in an inscription by Sennacherib, who expressly states that the divine command was procured through divination:[19]

a-[na pi]-i ša [d]šamaš u [d]adad	. . . at the word of Shamash and
ina bi-ri iq-bu-nim-ma	Adad (which) they spoke through
	extispicy

This is, however, only evidence that the divine word was sometimes given through the oracle and executed by the king in his deeds. It does not mean that the whole idea of the word as the instrument through which the deity exercises his control over the events of history can be reduced to the conception that the king acts upon answers attained by certain divination techniques. There are many passages in the texts where the divine word cannot possibly be interpreted as instructions

---

[17] Streck, *Assurbanipal* II, p. 240 ('Die Stele S[2]', ll. 4 ff.)

[18] On divination techniques and the significance of divination in Mesopotamia see e.g. the section 'The Arts of the Diviner' in Oppenheim, *Ancient Mesopotamia*, pp. 206 ff.

[19] Luckenbill, *The Annals of Sennacherib* (The University of Chicago Oriental Institute Publications, 2), Chicago 1924, p. 140 ('Inscription intended for a foundation stele (I 6)', ll. 8 f.). Cf. also l. 3 of the same inscription.

given through the omens. A very clear case is found in Esarhaddon's (680–669 B.C.) 'letter to the god'. During one of his campaigns the king besieged a city called Uppume, and had built a ramp. One night the defenders sprinkled the ramp with naphtha and tried to set it on fire. What then happened is described in the following manner (col. II, ll. 5 ff.):[20]

ina qi-bit ᵈ*marduk šar₄ ilâni*ᵐᵉˢ	At the order of Marduk, the king
i-[z]i-qam-ma ᵗᵘ₁₅*iltânu ma-nit*	of the gods, the north wind, the
*bêl ilâni*ᵐᵉˢ *ṭa-a-bu lišân* ᵈ*gira*	pleasant breeze of the lord of
mun-na-aḫ-[z]i a-na ᵘʳᵘ*up-pu-me*	the gods, blew and turned the
ú-sa-ḫir-ma ₍a₎₍ram₎*-mu*₍ ₍ul₎ ₍is₎-	tongue of the increasing[21] fire
[*bat?* xxx] *dûr-šú iq-mu-ma*	against Uppume; it did not
ú-še-me di-tal-liš	c[atch?] the ramp . . ., but burned
	down its (i.e. the city's) wall and
	laid it in ashes.

The divine command is here issued to the north wind; clearly it is not a question of an oracle obtained through divination. It might on the other hand be objected that when Marduk makes the wind blow in a certain direction, this is evidence of a divine power over nature rather than over history. But the important thing in the context is that this is a means of controlling *events* and so of governing the course of history. The successful attack against the city is the result of a divine intervention, and the medium through which the deity is said to have affected the events is his word. A passage in Ex. 14 springs into one's mind (v. 21):

ויולך יהוה את־הים ברוח קדים	And Yhwh drove the sea back by
עזה כל־הלילה וישם את־הים	a strong east wind the whole night
לחרבה ויבקעו המים:	and made the sea dry land, and
	the water was divided.

This divine intervention made it possible for the Israelites to walk on dry ground through the sea and so to escape the pursuing Egyptians,

---

[20] Borger, *Die Inschriften Asarhaddons*, p. 104.

[21] *munnaḫzi* (partic. N of *aḫāzu*) is interpreted in different ways by the editors and translators: H. Winckler has 'gefrässig' (*Altorientalische Forschungen*, 2: 1, Leipzig 1898, p. 33), Luckenbill 'devouring' (*Ancient Records of Assyria and Babylonia* II, 1927, p. 233), and Borger 'angefacht (?)' (op. cit., p. 104). The word seems to denote that the fire was beginning to burn up: cf. *CAD* s. v. *aḫāzu*: 'to flare up (said of fire)', and *AHw* s. v.: 'um sich greifen, sich ausbreiten, bes. v. Feuer'.

who perished in the returning water. Here too the divine power over the wind is used to govern events and to secure success. It is interesting to notice that it is in fact the non-biblical text that lays stress on the divine word: 'At the order of Marduk . . .', whereas the biblical account has simply 'And Yhwh drove . . .'!

A comparable instance is found in an interesting text from Babylonia, a 'Fürstenspiegel'[22] or 'Advice to a Prince',[23] warning the king against the divine retribution which threatens him if he 'does not heed justice'. The text belongs in the first centuries of the first millennium B.C.: F. M. T. Böhl attempts a precise dating and suggests the early years of the reign of Merodach-Baladan (721–710 B.C.),[24] whereas W. G. Lambert refrains from identifying the king for whom the cautions are meant and who 'need not have been an important figure historically': he was probably 'one of the kings of Babylon between 1000 and 700 B.C.'[25] The text gives a detailed account of the penalties which the gods will impose on an unjust ruler. These punishments are usually described as political or military disasters, so that the text is yet another testimony of the general idea of a divine control over historical events. Thus if the king accepts a bribe and improperly convicts a guiltless citizen, then[26]

^{d}en-líl bēl mātāti ^{lú}nakra	Enlil, the lord of the lands, will
a-ḫa-a-am i-da-kaš-šum-ma	levy a foreign enemy against him
ummānāti-šu ú-šam-qá-tì	and vanquish his army.

Similar things are also said about Marduk[27] and Era.[28] The important thing in this connexion, however, is that in one passage the disastrous events are said to be brought about by the word of the deity. Towards the end of the text the warnings are extended to the king's chief officers as well: if the counsellor or the general commit certain offences, the following punishments will come upon them (ll. 47 ff.):[29]

---

[22] F. M. T. Böhl, Der babylonische Fürstenspiegel (MAOG 11: 3), Leipzig 1937.

[23] The heading given to this text in Lambert, Babylonian Wisdom Literature, pp. 110 ff.

[24] Op. cit., p. 33.

[25] Op. cit., p. 111. Cf. now also I. M. Diakonoff, 'A Babylonian Political Pamphlet from about 700 B.C.', Studies in Honor of Benno Landsberger, Chicago 1965, pp. 343 ff., who argues that the warnings 'were addressed to Sennacherib in his early years (or possibly to his son Aššurnādinšumi)' (p. 346).

[26] Ll. 12 f.; Lambert, op. cit., p. 112.

[27] Ll. 17 f.; op. cit., p. 112.

[28] Ll. 36 f.; op. cit., p. 114.

[29] Op. cit., p. 114.

ina qi-bit ᵈé-a šàr apsî um-ma-an	at the order of Ea, the king of the
u šu-ut rēši ina [ᵍⁱ]ˢ*kakki imuttu*	subterranean ocean, the coun-
a-šar-šú-nu a-na na-me-⌈*e*⌉	sellor and the general will die by
[*i*]*k-ka-am-mar ar-kat₅!-sun*	the sword, their place will become
šá-a-ru i-tab-bal ep-šet-sun	a heap of ruins, the wind will
za-⌈*qi-qí*⌉*-iš im-man-ni*	carry away their remains, and
	their work will be delivered to
	the storm.

Obviously the word of the god, which is again described as an active factor in historical events, cannot here be equated with an oracle: it is thought of as a divine command which is shaping the events directly, without a human intermediary as the recipient of the order.

An interesting feature in the 'Advice to a Prince' is its striking formal resemblance to the omen texts.[30] The omen style is used effectively to give the cautions a general wording, avoiding any direct references to a particular king: 'If a king does not heed justice ...'. This way of beginning the sentence with a conditional clause is typical of omens (though curiously enough the introductory *šumma* 'if' is not expressed in this text, contrary to the characteristic omen formula). The author is dependent on the omen style in other respects as well, especially in the loose syntax and in some of the phraseology.[31] On the other hand Böhl[32] has emphasized a difference between this text and the omen literature: the typical magic pattern of the omens is here superseded by the ethical pattern of retribution and reward for evil and good deeds. One could add that the difference also concerns the relation between the incident mentioned in the conditional clause and the event described in the apodosis: in the omens the relation is that between portent and occurrence, with no clear idea of any causal connexion between the two, whereas here the relation is naturally that between cause and effect. Both these patterns, incidentally, seem to presuppose the idea of a divine power over the course of events: the very existence of omens implies, of course, both that the god is willing to communicate his intentions and that he controls the sequence of events predicted in the omen, just as the warnings to an unjust king in 'Advice to a Prince' are based on the conviction that the gods are able to shape the destiny of the ruler and thereby to punish or reward him.

The idea of the divine word as a motive force in history is in fact

---

[30] 'Formgeschichtlich gehört unser Text ... zur Omen-Literatur', Böhl, op. cit., p. 11. Cf. also Lambert, op. cit., p. 110.

[31] Lambert, loc. cit.

[32] Op. cit., p. 26.

also something which 'Advice to a Prince' seems to have in common with the omen literature. One instance is found in the class of omens which Oppenheim calls the 'empirical' group[34] and which contains material about historical incidents, though these cannot always be fitted into the pattern of events already known. In this group belongs an omen which tells about the 'destruction of Ur at the word of Sin', *ina amât* ^{d}*sin*.[35] This is probably, as Oppenheim points out, an allusion to the Elamite conquest, but quite apart from the question of how the event at which the text hints should be identified, it is certainly worth noticing that the word of the god is here clearly perceived as a causal factor in history.

A clear case where the stereotyped phrase 'at the order of (the god)' cannot refer to a divine instruction through the oracle to act in a certain manner is found in a passage in the annals of Sennacherib, in the complete version represented by 'the Oriental Institute Prism Inscription'. Toward the end of the account of the king's seventh campaign we read (col. V, ll. 11 ff.):[36]

i-na u₄-me-šu-ma i-na qí-bit	At that time, at the order of
^{d}*aššur bêli-ia* ^{1}*kudur-*^{d}*na-ḫu-un-du*	Ashur, my lord, Kudur-Nahundu,
šar ^{kur}*elamti*^{ki} *3 arḫê*^{meš} *ul*	the king of Elam, did not live
ú-mal-li-ma i-na u₄-me la	another (lit., did not fill) three
ši-im-ti-šú ur-ru-ḫi-iš im-tu-ut	months (but) died suddenly
	before his time.

Here the divine intervention through the word brings about the death of an enemy king, and the incident is even said to have occurred against the decree of destiny, which is otherwise also thought of as something ordained by the gods.[37] Perhaps, however, the expression *ina ûme la šimtišu*, lit., 'on a day not of his fate', means nothing more than 'prematurely', being used in a rather weakened sense, without conscious reference to the divinely decreed destiny. Though the passage just

---

[34] Oppenheim, 'Zur keilschriftlichen Omenliteratur', *Or* N.S. 5, 1936, pp. 219 ff.

[35] Op. cit., p. 220.

[36] Luckenbill, op. cit., p. 41.

[37] As, e.g., in the following passage from the annals of Ashurnasirpal II (883–859 B.C.): *ši-ma-a-te an-na-a-te ina pi-i ilâni*^{meš} *rabûti*^{meš} *ú-ṣa-ni-ma a-na ši-im-ti-ia ki-ni-iš ú-kin-nu* 'these destinies came forth out of the mouth of the great gods; they duly determined them as my destiny' (the text published in Budge–King, *Annals of the Kings of Assyria*, p. 266). For *aṣû ina pî* cf. Esarhaddon's 'Letter to the god', col. II, ll. 33 f., quoted below. On the meaning of *šimtu*, which is only inadequately expressed by the English 'destiny', see Oppenheim in *Ancient Mesopotamia*, pp. 201 ff.

quoted may possibly tell against it, one might otherwise connect the idea of the divine control of history through the word with the idea of the 'fixing of the fates', the conception that the gods decree the destinies of men and states. At least it seems natural so to interpret the following passage from the curses in the inscription of Adad-nirari I (1307–1275 B.C.):[38]

na-às-pu-uḫ ma-ti-šu ḫa-la-aq	Disintegration of his country,
ni-še-šu ù ku-du-ri-šu i-na	destruction of his people and of
pi-šu-nu kab-ti lu-ṣa-am-ma	his boundaries may proceed from their (i.e. the gods') worthy mouth.

The same expression recurs in Esarhaddon's so-called 'Letter to the god', col. II, ll. 33 f., where the king reports what he has written to an enemy ruler:[39]

ina pi-i ilâni[meš] šu-ut šamê erṣetim]	From the mouth of the gods of
[. . .]x it-ta-ṣa-a sa-pa-aḫ mâti-ka	heaven and earth . . . the disintegration of your country came forth.

Whether or not such passages allude to the yearly divine fixing of the destinies they do at any rate constitute evidence for the idea of the divine word as a motive power in the events of history. The texts quoted show this idea to have been current in different connexions: both whole chains of events and more isolated incidents are seen as the result of the god's intervention through his powerful word. That this conception is very similar to the one found in the Old Testament and studied by Grether and others should be obvious. The similarity in fact goes beyond the general view of the word as an 'active factor in history': there is sometimes also close agreement in the accounts of how the divine word functions in the course of events. In the so-called Rassam Cylinder we find a version of the annals of Assurbanipal, containing *inter alia* the following account of the sad lot of one of the king's adversaries (col. III, ll. 4 ff.):[40]

---

[38] Ebeling–Meissner–Weidner, op. cit., p. 66 (inscription no. 2, 'Die Fluchformel der Inschriften Adadnarâris I.' (so p. XXV), ll. 53 f.). The same formulation recurs on p. 98 (inscription no. 12, ll. 23 ff.).

[39] Borger's edition, op. cit., p. 105.

[40] Streck, *Assurbanipal* II, p. 24.

¹aḫ-še-e-ri la pa-liḫ bêlu-ti-ia i-na a-mat ᵈištar a-ši-bat ᵘʳᵘarba-ilu šá ultu re-e-ši taq-bu-ú um-ma ana-ku mi-tu-tu ¹aḫ-še-e-ri šár ᵏᵘʳman-na-a-a ki-i šá aq-bu-u ep-pu-uš ina qâtê⁽ᴵᴵ⁾ ardâni⁽ᵐᵉˢ⁾-šú tam-nu-šu-u-ma nišê⁽ᵐᵉˢ⁾ mâti-šú si-ḫu eli-šú ú-šab-šú-u ina sûqi āli-šú ˡᵘšá-lam-ta-šu id-du-u-šú in-da-áš-šá-ru ˡᵘpa-gar-šú

Ahsheri, who did not fear my lordship, at the word of Ishtar, dwelling in Arbela, which she had spoken from the beginning: 'The death of Ahsheri, king of the Mannai, I shall bring about as I have spoken'–into the hands of his servants she delivered him and the people of his land raised sedition against him. They threw his body into the street of his city and dragged his corpse (on the ground).

The combination of the divine prediction and its fulfilment in the actual course of events is strongly reminiscent of the Deuteronomist's technique of stressing the correspondence between prediction and realization,[41] as for instance in the story of the death of Jezebel (which, incidentally, agrees in several details with Ashurbanipal's account of Ahsheri's miserable end). In 2 Kings 9 the Deuteronomist makes Jehu comment upon the queen's death: when he hears the report of those who went to bury her, he says (vv. 36 f.):

דבר־יהוה הוא אשר דבר ביד־עבדו
אליהו התשבי לאמר בחלק יזרעאל
יאכלו הכלבים את־בשר איזבל:
והית נבלת איזבל כדמן על־פני
השדה בחלק יזרעאל

This is the word of Yhwh which he spoke through his servant Eliah the Tishbite, saying: 'In the tract of Jezreel the dogs shall eat the flesh of Jezebel; and the corpse of Jezebel shall be as dung upon the field in the tract of Jezreel ...'

Both in Ashurbanipal's account and in that of the Deuteronomist it is of course not just a prediction that comes true; the divine word not only contains information about things which are to happen: it is the very force which governs the course of events.[42] This is, to quote again Grether's phrase, 'das Wort als wirksamer Faktor', and both in the Akkadian and in the Hebrew text it concerns historical events.

---

[41] See G. von Rad, *Deuteronomiumstudien* (FRLANT N.F. 40), Göttingen 1947, part B: 'Die deuteronomistische Geschichtstheologie in den Königsbüchern', pp. 54 ff. (=*Gesammelte Studien zum Alten Testament* (ThB 8), München 1958, pp. 192 ff.), and the same author's *Theologie des Alten Testaments* 1, München 1957, pp. 338 ff.
[42] von Rad speaks of 'das geschichtsschöpferische Wort', e.g. in *Theologie des AT* 1, p. 342.

The evidence that the idea of the divine word as a motive power in history occurs also outside the Old Testament has so far been taken from Sumerian and Akkadian texts. Again instances can be found also in other parts of Israel's environment. An example from a Hittite source may suffice to illustrate this. The famous 'Apology of Hattusilis' (i.e. Hattusilis III, 1275–1250 B.C.), one of the most distinctive and interesting documents from the Hittite Empire,[43] repeatedly declares that certain events happened 'at the command of the god'—the same phrase which we have met in so many Akkadian texts. Here too it may in some cases be just a way of expressing the fact that the omens had been consulted before a military campaign, as when Hattusilis begins an account of his royal brother's difficulties with rebellious neighbours in the following manner (col. I, ll. 75 f.):

When, however, my brother Muwattallis at the command of his (patron) deity went down to the Lower Country and left Hattusas, . . .[44]

But this interpretation seems out of the question in other cases, as for instance in the following passage, describing how Hattusilis' nephew, king Urhi-Teshub, having succeeded his father Muwatallis, attempted to reduce his uncle's provinces (col. III, ll. 56 ff.):

He took away from me all (my) subjects; Samuhas[45] also he took away from me; the depopulated lands also that I had settled again, all those too he took away from me, and he made me weak. Hakpissas,[46] however, according to the command of a god he did not take away from me.[47]

This is clearly an allusion to a divine word which is capable of governing the course of events.

It is rather surprising, in the light of the ample evidence from extra-biblical sources, that it has been possible to argue that the idea of the god's word as a creative factor in history is found only in the Old

---

[43] On this text see further below, pp. 110 f.

[44] Sturtevant–Bechtel, *A Hittite Chrestomathy*, p. 69. The passage is also found in Goetze, *Hattušiliš. Der Bericht über seine Thronbesteigung nebst den Paralleltexten* (MVAG 29: 3), Leipzig 1925, pp. 14 f. (Hittite text and German translation).

[45] A city in the eastern part of the realm.

[46] The capital of the north-eastern provinces where Hattusilis had resided as governor under his brother, king Muwatallis. Cf. Gurney, *The Hittites*, p. 35.

[47] Sturtevant–Bechtel, op. cit., p. 77. Cf. Goetze, op. cit., pp. 28 f., who has 'auf Geheiss der Gottheit'. In a later publication, *Neue Bruchstücke zum grossen Text des Hattušiliš und den Paralleltexten* (MVAG 34: 2), Leipzig 1930, p. 29, Goetze gives the translation 'auf Geheiss (seiner) Gottheit'.

Testament. The explanation seems to be that both Grether and Dürr when examining texts outside the Old Testament restricted themselves to hymns praising the power of the divine word, whereas Grether especially used all sorts of Old Testament texts, both historical and others, as sources when he collected the evidence for the biblical view. Had the study of the comparative material been extended to the same literary categories, the result would obviously—as is evident from the above—have been different. And conversely: if the Old Testament material is taken only from poetical eulogies of the divine word, the resultant picture is rather reminiscent of that drawn by Grether to describe the extra-biblical idea. The passages in the Psalter which praise the creative power of Yhwh's word do in fact connect it precisely with 'Weltentstehung' and 'Naturgeschehen', which Grether found characteristic of the non-biblical religious texts from the ancient Near East,[48] as for instance in Ps. 33.6 ff.:

בדבר יהוה שמים נעשו	By the word of Yhwh the heavens were made,
וברוח פיו כל־צבאם:	and all their host by the breath of his mouth.
כנס כנד מי הים	He gathers the waters of the sea as in a water-skin;[49]
נתן באצרות תהומות:	he puts the deep in storehouses.
ייראו מיהוה כל־הארץ	Let all the earth fear Yhwh,
ממנו יגורו כל־ישבי תבל:	let all the inhabitants of the world stand in awe of him!
כי הוא אמר ויהי	For he spoke, and it came to be;
הוא־צוה ויעמד:	he commanded, and it stood forth.

or in Ps. 147.15 ff.:

השלח אמרתו ארץ	He sends forth his command upon earth;
עד־מהרה ירוץ דברו:	his word runs swiftly.
הנתן שלג כצמר	He gives snow like wool;
כפור כאפר יפזר:	he spreads rime like ashes.
משליך קרחו כפתים	He casts forth his ice like morsels;

---

[48] Grether, op. cit., p. 139; cf. above, p. 54.

[49] Read נֹד = נאֹד 'water-skin', for MT's נֵד 'heap, barrier', with LXX, Peshitta, Targum and others; cf. BH³, KBL, and the commentaries.

לפני קרתו מי יעמד׃   before his cold the waters cease
to flow.[50]

ישלח דברו וימסם   He sends forth his word and
melts them;

ישב רוחו יזלו־מים׃   he makes his wind blow, and the
waters flow.

In such passages the psalmists' dependence on a common ancient Near Eastern tradition is evident:[51] we have to do here with an ancient *motif* represented already in old Sumerian and Akkadian hymns. Therefore it is hardly correct, as Grether seems to maintain,[52] that the Israelite ideas of the efficacy of the divine word at the creation and in the process of nature have developed from a more original conception of this word as a motive power in history, with a minimum of influence from the environment. Rather it would seem that both conceptions are very ancient in the Semitic religions, and that Israel has here a share in a common heritage; it is not probable that in the Old Testament one is older and more original than the other. And again the very distinction between nature and history seems little relevant and is not likely to have been recognized at all: to the peoples of the ancient Near East the word of the god was a mighty and terrifying power which could prove effective in all spheres of life, a dynamic force bringing about the death or victories of kings as well as the growth or withering of the crops. The power of the divine word knows no bounds; its effects can be traced in nature and history alike. The ancient Israelites knew this; Sumerians and Babylonians, Assyrians and Hittites knew it as well.

---

[50] Read מים יעמדו 'the waters cease moving', for MT's מי יעמד 'who can stand?'; cf. BH³; D. W. Thomas, *The Text of the Revised Psalter,* London 1963, p. 55; H.-J. Kraus, *Psalmen* 2 (BKAT XV/2), Neukirchen 1960, ad. loc.

[51] Cf. Kraus, op. cit., p. 958: 'In Israel sind die altorientalischen Vorstellungen von der schöpferischen Macht des göttlichen Wortes auf Jahwe übertragen worden'.

[52] Op. cit., p. 144.

CHAPTER FIVE

The Divine Plan in History

The idea that the deity acts in history is not peculiarly Israelite, as the previous chapters have shown. But there is another way of defining the distinctive Old Testament view of history, often put forward by authors who have avoided the too simple contrast between the Israelite belief in the divine control of events and the general Near Eastern conception of the divine activity in the realm of nature. It is said that when Yhwh acts in history, unlike the heathen gods he does so according to definite plan. This view is expressed with characteristic clarity by Lindblom in his work on the Old Testament prophets: 'nothing like the prophetic idea of the history of Israel as the realization of a fixed divine plan from its beginning to its end is to be found elsewhere in the ancient world.'[1] Another example of the same attempt to find the typically Israelite in the idea of a divine plan in history is found in Jacob's study of the historical tradition in Israel: he describes the Old Testament prophets as 'ceux qui, pour la première fois dans l'antiquité, ont envisagé l'histoire universelle comme le déroulement d'un plan divin.'[2]

As a rule the divine plan in history is referred to in rather general terms: we are not told the precise import of this idea, nor the evidence for it in the text of the Old Testament. It is put forward as something obvious and universally known that the idea of God's plan determines the Israelite view of history. This may be observed also in O. Cullmann's latest great work, *Heil als Geschichte:* when Cullmann deals

---

[1] *Prophecy in Ancient Israel*, p. 325. Cf. the same author's formulation in an earlier paper on Israelite historiography: 'Man uppfattade skeendet, närmast i det egna folkets historia, såsom ett handlande av Gud, och därtill ett handlande efter en bestämd plan, med ett bestämt syfte och mot ett bestämt mål.' ('Historieskrivningen i Israel och dess ställning inom forntidens hävdateckning', STK 11, 1935, p. 222). In a preliminary sketch of the present work, a paper read to the Finnish Exegetical Society in 1965 (subsequently printed in *TATT* 71, 1966, pp. 13 ff.), I still quoted this view with assent (op. cit., pp. 33 f.). The present chapter constitutes my second thoughts on the subject.

[2] *La tradition historique en Israël*, p. 135.

with the Old Testament background of the New Testament statements about a divine *Heilsplan,* he speaks very generally and as a matter of course about 'the divine plan' in the Old Testament.[3] It is interesting to note that in this connexion he refers to one single work only, Fichtner's article on Yhwh's plan in Isaiah's message[4]—and not without reason: there seems to be no special study of the subject other than this short essay which does not examine the concept of the divine plan in the whole Israelite literature but, as the title indicates, only in Isaiah.

Fichtner, too, takes for granted that the idea of Yhwh's plan in history occupies a prominent place in the message of the Old Testament. In the view of the prophets, God is active in history 'und verfolgt einen bestimmten Plan. Das Wissen um diesen Tatbestand steht im Grunde hinter der gesamten prophetischen Verkündigung des Alten Testaments'.[5] Having proclaimed that the idea of God's plan is of such fundamental importance to the entire prophetic preaching in the Old Testament, Fichtner makes, however, some noteworthy reservations. He mentions Isaiah's precursors, Amos and Hosea. The message of Amos, too, is based on the assurance that God follows a plan in his dealings with his people, but Fichtner admits that this is nowhere put into words by Amos: 'Eine präzise Formulierung für das Planvolle Handeln Jahves nach festem Ratschluss findet sich jedoch bei Amos noch nicht.'[6] It is the same with Hosea: the idea that Yhwh acts according to a fixed plan is somehow to be apprehended from his message, but 'er selbst spricht es nie expressis verbis aus'.[7] This sort of argument is of course dangerous: how can we know that Amos and Hosea did in fact hold this view if it is nowhere expressed in the texts?[8] It appears that an examination of the Old Testament idea of a divine plan in history, its occurrence and meaning, may not be out of place.

It seems appropriate first to find out whether the term itself occurs in the Old Testament: is the expression 'God's plan' or 'Yhwh's plan' used by its authors? The first problem is that of the equivalent of 'plan' in biblical Hebrew. There is hardly a Hebrew term whose field of

---

[3] *Heil als Geschichte. Heilsgeschichtliche Existenz im Neuen Testament,* Tübingen 1965, pp. 71 f.

[4] J. Fichtner, 'Jahves Plan in der Botschaft des Jesaja', *ZAW* 63 (N.F. 22), 1951, pp. 16 ff.

[5] Op. cit., p. 16.

[6] Loc. cit.

[7] Op. cit., p. 17.

[8] I am, of course, aware that the basic conceptions of an author are not always explicitly stated. But before one can maintain that an idea is 'im Grunde' implied by an author, it must be shown to be prerequisite to his message, and I cannot find that Fichtner has done this.

meaning covers entirely that of the English word, but in certain connexions עצה seems to denote the same as 'plan'. In most cases עצה means, of course, 'counsel, advice', but it has a wider and less specific meaning than the words to which it most nearly corresponds in our modern western languages, and we must resort to a whole series of terms to cover the different shades of עצה: 'counsel', 'advice', 'consultation', 'purpose', and also 'plan'.

Ps. 20.5, for instance, seems to be a case where עצה clearly means 'plan'. In a prayer for the king it says:

יתן־לך כלבבך	May he (i.e. Yhwh) grant you your heart's desire
וכל־עצתך ימלא:	and fulfil all your plans.

Another example is found in Jer. 49.30 b:

כי־יעץ עליכם נבוכדראצר	For Nebuchadrezzar king of
מלך־בבל עצה וחשב עליהם	Babylon has devised a plan
מחשבה:	against you and made a design against you.

These instances, however, concern human plans, and the next question is whether עצה is used in the Old Testament to denote a divine plan. As far as I am aware there are about a dozen such passages.

Four of these occur in the Book of Isaiah, though in different parts of this collection of oracles from diverse ages and authors. Two seem to be Isaianic. In Isa. 5.19 the prophet's adversaries are depicted, those who mock his predictions of the impending judgement,

האמרים ימהר יחישה מעשהו	... those who say, 'Let him make
למען נראה ותקרב ותבואה עצת	speed and hasten his work that
קדוש ישראל ונדעה:	we may see it, let what the Holy One of Israel has planned draw near and come, that we may know it.'

The expression עצת קדוש ישראל, translated in RSV 'the purpose of the Holy One of Israel', refers to something which the God of Israel, according to Isaiah, has threatened to do, and seems to come at least very close to the meaning 'plan'.

The second passage in Isaiah is 14.24 ff.[9] Here the prophet proclaims Yhwh's purpose to destroy the Assyrian conqueror in Palestine:

---

[9] The section 14.24–27 has often been regarded as the work of a later author, but the reasons against its genuineness are not decisive; in fact 'In dem ganzen Stück ist kein Wort, das nicht von Jes. sein könnte.' (B. Duhm, *Das Buch Jesaja übersetzt und erklärt* (HKAT III: 1), 4. Aufl., Göttingen 1922, ad loc.). Cf. also O. Eissfeldt,

נשבע יהוה צבאות לאמר אם־לא   Yhwh of hosts has sworn: 'Surely
כאשר דמיתי כן היתה וכאשר   as I have thought, so shall it be,
יעצתי היא תקום: לשבר אשור   and as I have purposed, so shall
בארצי ועל־הרי אבוסנו וסר   it come to pass, (25) that I will
מעליהם עלו וסבלו מעל שכמו   break Ashur in my land, and
יסור: זאת העצה היעוצה על־   trample him on my mountains;
כל־הארץ וזאת היד הנטויה   and his yoke shall depart from
על־כל־הגוים: כי־יהוה צבאות   them, and his burden depart from
יעץ ומי יפר וידו הנטויה ומי   his shoulder.' (26) This is the
ישיבנה: purpose that is purposed against
the whole earth; and this is the
hand that is stretched out against
all the nations. (27) For Yhwh
of hosts has purposed and who
will annul it? His hand is stretched
out, and who will turn it back?

Besides the noun עצה we find here also the corresponding verb יעץ
used about Yhwh. Again it is difficult to judge precisely which shade of
meaning is intended. The translation of עצה and יעץ used above, 'purpose', is that found in AV as well as in RSV. 'Decision' and 'decide'
would also be possible, and 'plan'[10] is perhaps better still: in this passage
too the prophet refers to the designs of Yhwh. 'Here Isaiah's message
that Yahweh is Lord of history, and that his purpose is the finally
determining factor in what happens, comes to clear expression.'[11]

The so-called Isaiah Apocalypse also contains the word עצה used of
divine plans. In a thanksgiving for the overthrow of an enemy city it
says (25.1):

יהוה אלהי אתה   Yhwh, thou art my God;
ארוממך אודה שמך   I will exalt thee, I will praise
thy name;
כי עשית פלא עצות   for thou hast carried out
wondrous plans,[12]
מרחוק אמונה אמן: from afar, in perfect faithfulness.

Einleitung in das Alte Testament unter Einschluss der Apokryphen und Pseudepigraphen sowie der apokryphen- und pseudepigraphenartigen Qumrān-Schriften, 3.,
neubearb. Aufl., Tübingen 1964, p. 420.

[10] So G. B. Gray, A Critical and Exegetical Commentary on the Book of Isaiah
I–XXXIX (ICC), I, Edinburgh 1912, in his translation of this passage (p. 262).

[11] R. B. Y. Scott, 'Isaiah Chapters 1–39. Introduction and Exegesis', IB 5, New York–
Nashville 1956, ad. loc.

[12] So against the accents in MT, with BH³ and most commentaries. RSV follows the
masoretes: 'for thou hast done wonderful things, plans formed of old, faithful and
sure.'

This is also a testimony of the idea of Yhwh's purposes in history and of his power to accomplish what he has decided to do.

Deutero-Isaiah, too, uses the word עֵצָה in a context where it refers to God's plan in history. In 46.10 Yhwh speaks:

אמר עצתי תקום ... saying, 'My plan shall be fulfilled,

וכל־חפצי אעשה: and I will do all my pleasure ...',

and in the following verse Cyrus is called אִישׁ עֲצָתוֹ 'the man of my counsel', i.e. the one who will execute my plan. Both 'purpose', 'counsel', and 'plan' seem possible as renderings of עֵצָה in Isa. 46.10.

Besides these four passages in the Book of Isaiah there are three further instances in the prophets. In Mi. 4.12[13] it is said of the pagan nations:

והמה לא ידעו מחשבות יהוה But they do not know Yhwh's
ולא הבינו עצתו כי קבצם thoughts, they do not understand
כעמיר גרנה: his plan: that he has gathered
them as sheaves to the threshing
floor.[14]

Again, 'purpose' may also be a possible rendering of עֵצָה: the nations do not understand what Yhwh has in mind, what he is going to do with them.

The two remaining instances of עֵצָה used about a divine plan in the Old Testament are both found in the book of Jeremiah, in 49.20 and 50.45, among the oracles of doom on foreign nations. The formulation is identical in both cases;[15] only the name of the enemy people varies. In 49.20 we hear about

---

[13] This passage belongs to a section which is generally, and probably rightly, regarded as secondary (cf. the commentaries), though it is difficult to be quite as confident about this as most commentators seem to be.

[14] H. Gottlieb, 'Den tærskende kvie – Mi 4, 11–13', *DTT* 26, 1963, pp. 167 ff., maintains that the metaphorical language used here must have its origin in the cult, in a holy 'ritual threshing'. This seems to me wholly improbable and an outcrop of the very one-sided but not uncommon tendency to assume that almost everything in the Old Testament must have had its origin in the cult. Is it altogether improbable that a prophet in an agricultural people could have come to use the metaphor of threshing without the intermediation of the cult?

[15] The problem of the mutual relation of these passages and their genuineness is very complicated. Most commentators think that 49.19–21 has been adapted from 50.44–46: the expressions used to depict the reaction at the overthrow of the enemy are held to be more appropriate to the fall of Babylon than to the fall of Edom (so e.g. W. Rudolph, *Jeremia* (HAT I: 12), 2. Aufl., Tübingen 1958, ad loc.; J. P.

עצת־יהוה אשר יעץ אל־אדום	... Yhwh's plan which he has
ומחשבותיו אשר חשב אל־ישבי	made against Edom and his
תימן	purposes which he has purposed
	against the inhabitants of Teman,

whereas 50.45 speaks about

עצת־יהוה אשר יעץ אל־בבל	... Yhwh's plan which he has
ומחשבותיו אשר חשב אל־ארץ	made against Babylon and his
כשדים	purposes which he has purposed
	against the land of the Chaldeans.

RSV's choice of 'plan' to render עצה in these two passages seems
justified.

Two instances of עצה in the Psalms must also be discussed in this
connexion. The first case is Ps. 33.10 f., where the word occurs twice,
being used both of men and of Yhwh:

יהוה הפיר עצת־גוים	Yhwh brought the plan of the
	nations to nought;
הניא מחשבות עמים:	he frustrated the thoughts of the
	peoples.
עצת יהוה לעולם תעמד	But Yhwh's plan stands for ever[16]
מחשבות לבו לדר ודר:	the thoughts of his heart for all
	generations

'The counsel of the nations' (RSV) refers in all probability to hostile
plans against the people of God, and so it seems more natural to take
עצת יהוה as an expression for that divine plan which ultimately controls the course of history[17] in spite of all human planning and con-
spiring.

It is more doubtful if עצה has this meaning in Ps. 106.13. In a retrospect of the history of Israel it is said of the apostate people:

Hyatt, 'The Book of Jeremiah. Introduction and Exegesis', *IB* 5, New York–Nashville
1956, ad loc.). To what extent these oracles may derive ultimately from Jeremiah is
difficult and perhaps impossible to decide: the material in these prophecies against
foreign nations is likely to have been reshaped and expanded by traditionists for
several generations.

[16] A similar phrase occurs also in Prov. 19: 21: 'Many are the devices in a man's
heart, but it is Yhwh's plan that will stand', ועצת יהוה היא תקום. This seems,
however, to be little more than a Hebrew version of 'man proposes, God disposes'
(cf. Prov. 16.9), and nothing is really said of a divine plan in history.

[17] Cf. Kraus, *Psalmen* 1, ad loc.: 'so ist עצת־יהוה die fortwaltende Geschichts-
macht.'

מהרו שכחו מעשיו   They soon forgot his works;

לא־חכו לעצתו: they did not wait for his counsel.

Kraus comments: 'Doch eigenartig ist der Hinweis auf Jahwes עצה. Gemeint ist der „Heilsplan" Gottes',[18] but it may be questioned whether this is not to read too much into the text. What the psalmist refers to is the murmuring of the people in the wilderness: they did not trust Yhwh to appease their hunger and thirst, and the expression probably means something like 'they did not bother to wait for God to find some expedient.'[19]

As far as I have been able to discover, these are all the passages where עצה is used of a divine plan in history.[20] But עצה is not, of course, the only word for 'plan' in the Hebrew language. There is another word of the same root, מועצה, which may have the same signification, but in the Old Testament it is used only of human plans, never of divine. In some of the Old Testament quotations above עצה was found in parallelism with מחשבה 'thought, device', and there are two more passages in the Book of Jeremiah where מחשבה refers to a divine plan. The first of these passages consists of the well-known words in Jeremiah's letter to the exiles in Babylon, 29.11:[21]

כי אנכי ידעתי את־המחשבת   For I know the thoughts that I

אשר אנכי חשב עליכם נאם־יהוה   have for you, says Yhwh, thoughts

מחשבות שלום ולא לרעה לתת   of peace, and not of evil, to give

לכם אחרית ותקוה: you the future you hope for.

Here מחשבת may as well be translated 'plans' (as in RSV): obviously the passage is about the designs that Yhwh has for the future of his people.

The second passage is Jer. 51.29. In a prophecy of doom against Babylon it says:[22]

---

[18] *Psalmen* 2, ad loc.

[19] Cf. Gunkel's understanding of this passage in his commentary: 'sie vermochten in ihrer Ungeduld nicht auf die Hilfe zu warten, womit Gottes Ratschluss ihre Not stillen würde.' (*Die Psalmen übersetzt und erklärt* (HKAT II: 2), 4. Aufl., Göttingen 1926, ad loc.)

[20] Isa. 19.17 might conceivably also be mentioned, but there עצה means rather 'decision' than 'plan' (AV: 'counsel'; RSV: 'purpose'). Cf. v. 12 (יעץ).

[21] Jer. 29.10 f. has sometimes been considered secondary by modern critics (e.g. P. Volz, *Der Prophet Jeremia übersetzt und erklärt* (KAT 10), Leipzig–Erlangen 1922, ad loc.), but without sufficient reason: see Rudolph, op. cit., ad loc.

[22] It is most doubtful if this passage can be regarded as genuine: cf. above, p. 72, n. 15.

ותרעש הארץ ותחל כי קמה	The land trembles and writhes
על־בבל מחשבות יהוה לשום	(in pain), for Yhwh's plans against
את־ארץ בבל לשמה מאין יושב:	Babylon are fulfilled: to make the land of Babylon a desolation, without inhabitant.

Another noun with a similar shade of meaning is מזמה, which usually denotes a design to the disadvantage of somebody, a hostile device. This word too is used a few times about Yhwh; primarily three passages from the Book of Jeremiah are of interest here. Denouncing the false prophets, Jeremiah says in 23.20:

לא ישוב אף־יהוה עד־עשתו ועד־	Yhwh's anger will not return until
הקימו מזמות לבו באחרית הימים	he has executed and accomplished
תתבוננו בה בינה:	the intents of his heart; in the latter days you will certainly understand it.

The same phrase is repeated in 30.24 in a partly different context.[23] In 51.11[24] the word מזמה is used about the divine plans for vengeance against Babylonia:

העיר יהוה את־רוח מלכי מדי	Yhwh has raised up the spirit of
כי־על־בבל מזמתו להשחיתה	the kings of the Medes, for his
כי־נקמת יהוה היא נקמת היכלו:	device is against Babylon, to destroy it; for that is Yhwh's vengeance, the vengeance for his temple.[25]

The word דרך should perhaps also be considered as a possible Hebrew term for the divine 'plan'. At any rate this is how Kraus wants to interpret Ps. 103.7:

יודיע דרכיו למשה	He made known his ways to Moses,
לבני ישראל עלילותיו:	his acts to the children of Israel.

---

[23] Jer. 23.20 is certainly genuine; 30.24 may be taken from this passage: cf. Rudolph, op. cit., ad loc.

[24] I.e. in a chapter with prophecies of doom against foreign nations, a section of doubtful genuineness: cf. above, p. 72, n. 15.

[25] A further instance of מזמה used of God should perhaps also be mentioned here: Job's answer to Yhwh's discourse out of the whirlwind begins (42.2): 'I know that thou canst do all things, and that no plan is impossible for thee' (ולא־יבצר ממך מזמה; cf. KBL s. v. III בצר.). But there is no idea of a divine plan in history here.

Kraus' commentary on this passage runs: 'דרך ist hier der Plan, die Führung . . . Mose gilt als Prophet, dem die Taten an Israel zuvor kund-gegeben wurden.'[26] The parallel passages which Kraus adduces in sup-port of his interpretation (Ex. 33.13; Deut. 32.4; Isa. 55.8 f.; 58.2; Ps. 18.31) are, however, inconclusive; only one of them is possibly relevant: Ex. 33.13, where Moses appeals to God:

וְעַתָּה אִם־נָא מָצָאתִי חֵן בְּעֵינֶיךָ	Now therefore, if I have found
הוֹדִעֵנִי נָא אֶת־דְּרָכֶךָ וְאֵדָעֵךָ	favour in thy sight, show me now
	thy ways that I may know thee . . .

It is perhaps conceivable that דְּרָכֶךָ could mean 'thy plans'. But in Ps. 103.7 the parallelism of 'ways' and 'acts' is an argument in favour of the interpretation of 'ways' as 'mode of action', God's 'moral ad-ministration',[27] and doubtless this understanding of the word gives a better meaning also in Ex. 33.13.[28]

These are, I believe, all the terms which may be considered as possible Hebrew equivalents of the word 'plan', and the passages quoted are those in which a divine 'plan' is expressly mentioned in the Old Testament. It seems appropriate here to look at these sayings a little closer, to recapitulate their contents and to find out what precisely they tell us about Yhwh's plan. The distribution of these passages is perhaps what first attracts attention: of the eleven statements (counting Jer. 49.20＝50.45 and 23.20＝30.24 as one each) which directly mention God's 'plan', five are found in the Book of Jeremiah, four in the Book of Isaiah, one in the Book of Micah and one in the Psalter. Thus the passages are concentrated in a small number of books, above all in prophetical writings. The expression as such is obviously not used by the majority of the Old Testament authors. Moreover, what we meet here is not *the* divine plan: these passages clearly do not speak of one and the same plan (a few of them indeed use the plural form). And we are not in fact told very much about God's plan(s). In some cases the expression is used about Yhwh's impending judgment of the heathen (five instances: Isa. 14.26; Mi. 4.12; Jer. 49.20＝50.45; 51.11, 29), in other connexions about his intention to afflict his own people (two instances: Isa. 5.19; Jer. 23.20＝30.24), and in one case about a visita-tion which has already befallen a hostile power (Isa. 25.1). It is further

---

[26] *Psalmen* 2, ad loc.

[27] BDB s. v. Cf. Gunkel, *Die Psalmen*, ad loc.: 'sein Walten'.

[28] Cf. Noth, *Das zweite Buch Mose. Exodus. Übersetzt und erklärt* (ATD 5), Göttingen 1959, ad loc.: Moses requests to be informed by Yhwh 'was er überhaupt vorhabe (in diesem allgemeinen Sinne sind wohl die „Wege" Gottes in V. 13a gemeint)'.

said that God's plan is sure, that it will stand for ever (Isa. 46.10 f.; Ps. 33.11), and finally we hear of a plan, the goal of which is the future welfare of Israel (Jer. 29.11).

Now the word 'plan' may of course have several somewhat different meanings. It may be used in a more pregnant sense about a more or less detailed scheme of action, or, to quote the *Oxford English Dictionary*, 'a formulated or organized method according to which something is to be done', 'the way in which it is proposed to carry out some proceeding'. But often the word is used also in a weakened sense, and then it may come very close to meaning 'purpose, intention'. It seems clear that when the word 'plan' is employed in the English translations of the Old Testament passages quoted above, it is never used in the first, pregnant sense. That Yhwh has a plan means nothing more than that he intends something by what he does, that he carries out his purposes, both in mercy and in punishment. To conclude: in the passages where a divine 'plan' is expressly mentioned, the words used do not have a pregnant or a more precise meaning but are fairly vague and wide terms; moreover they are used of several divine intentions. Not one of these passages can be quoted in support of the alleged Old Testament 'idea of the history of Israel as the realization of a fixed divine plan from its beginning to its end'.[29]

So far we have only studied passages where the very noun 'plan' is directly used. There are of course several passages in the Old Testament where verbs from the same roots as the nouns discussed above are used and where the English verb 'plan' (in a rather loose sense) may be a reasonable rendering. Some of the instances are included among the passages quoted above, as these nouns and the corresponding verbs occur often together in a *figura etymologica* meaning 'to make a plan'; other cases state only that God intends to do this or that (e.g. Jer. 26.3; 36.3; Mi. 2.3, all חשב), but as far as I am aware there is not a single case where they serve to express the idea of a divine plan in history in a proper sense.

But it is of course possible that the Old Testament authors may have something to say about a divine plan in history without using the term—the *matter* may well be there even if the *word* is not found. Our next task must therefore be to discover if there are any such passages.

An important group of material in this connexion is the J stratum in the Pentateuch, the Yahwistic traditions. Perhaps it is not so much individual statements in the narrative of the Yahwist (though I shall soon discuss some such passages) as rather the very composition and

---

[29] Cf. above, p. 68.

tendency that are relevant here. There is hardly any doubt that one of the most important features in J is precisely the historical perspective. Everything that happens, the entire sequence of occurrences, is depicted from a definite point of view: the course of events is not governed by blind forces or by despotic rulers but by the God of Israel, who controls the destinies of the world according to his will, even when it appears as if human wickedness, deceit and cruelty were the only motive forces in history. It may reasonably be asserted that this very perspective in J, the description of the chain of events as a *Führungsgeschichte,* gives us the right to speak here of a kind of divine plan in history, even if the term itself is never employed and we must, besides, use the word 'plan' in a weakened and rather wide sense.

But at least one important problem remains when we have established this: two different alternatives of interpretation must be taken into account. According to one view, the Yahwist surveys past history, traces out the divine 'plan' so to speak from the viewpoint of a result already arrived at: he discerns the divine guidance of the course of history after the event, from his outlook in the days of the Solomonic empire. According to another interpretation his theology of history contains also a hope for the future, an idea of a divine plan for events to come and a universal perspective: the Yahwist is then supposed to give a 'Gesamtdeutung des überlieferten Pentateucherzählungsstoffes als einer „Heilsgeschichte", d.h. einer Erzählung von einem geschichtlich konkreten göttlichen Handeln, das auf eine noch künftige Segnung „aller Sippen der bewohnten Erde", d.h. der Gesamtmenschheit, hinauswill und sich dazu Israels als Werkzeugs bedient'.[30] The choice between these two alternatives is largely dependent on the interpretation of the well-known words to Abraham in Gen. 12.3, and therefore we must pay some attention to this key passage in the Yahwist's narrative.[31] These are the words of the divine command to Abraham (12.1 ff.):

לך־לך מארצך וממולדתך ומבית
אביך אל־הארץ אשר אראך:
ואעשך לגוי גדול ואברכך ואגדלה
שמך והיה ברכה:

Go from your country, and from your kindred, and from your father's house, to the land that I will show you. And I will make of you a great nation, and I will bless you, and make your name great; and you shall be a blessing.

---

[30] Noth, *Überlieferungsgeschichte des Pentateuch,* Stuttgart 1948, pp. 256 f.
[31] That the beginning of Gen. 12 belongs to the Yahwistic tradition is generally agreed: see e.g. Eissfeldt, *Hexateuch-Synopse . . .,* Leipzig 1922, p. 19* (L+J); Noth, op. cit., p. 29.

ואברכה מברכיך ומקללך אאר
ונברכו בך כל משפחת
האדמה:

And I will bless those who bless
you, and him who curses you I
will curse; and by you all the
families of the earth shall bless
themselves.

The crucial word is נברכו: the rendering depends on the question
whether this Niphal form has a passive sense, as presupposed by AV:
'shall be blessed', or a reflective sense, as the translators of RSV have
preferred: 'shall bless themselves' (the passive rendering is there given
as an alternative in a footnote). The problem is not altogether easy to
solve, and the commentators, as is well known, are far from agreed.
If the passive translation is preferred—and many distinguished scholars
can be quoted in support of this solution—the passage acquires a universalistic tendency: according to God's plan Abraham is chosen as an
instrument of the divine blessing which shall reach all the nations of
the earth through him. Procksch's commentary on the passage is characteristic of this kind of exposition: 'Weil Jahwe seinen Geschichtsplan
an Abrams Person bindet, hängt der göttliche Segen und Fluch der
Menschheit—an Israel ist nicht gedacht—von ihrer inneren Stellung zur
Glaubensgestalt Abrams ab. Während Abrams Geschichte unterwegs
Segen und Fluch herbeiführt, ist das universale Ziel lauter Segen.'[32]
A similar interpretation is represented by among others S. R. Driver,[33] G.
von Rad,[34] J. Schreiner,[35] and H. W. Wolff.[36] When all is said and done,
however, the evidence appears to be in favour of the translation 'shall
bless themselves'. 'To bless oneself in someone('s name)' or 'by naming
someone' means to mention the name of someone as a benediction
according to the custom attested in the Old Testament, for instance
when Jacob blesses the sons of Joseph, saying (Gen. 48.20):

---

[32] O. Procksch, *Die Genesis übersetzt und erklärt* (KAT 1), 2. und 3. Aufl., Leipzig
und Erlangen 1924, ad loc.
[33] *The Book of Genesis with Introduction and Notes* (WC), 12th ed., London 1926,
ad. loc. (though apparently not without hesitation: 'If this rend. is correct,...').
[34] *Das erste Buch Mose. Genesis Kapitel 1–12, 9* (ATD 2), Göttingen 1949, ad loc.
[35] 'Segen für die Völker in der Verheissung an die Väter', *BZ* N.F. 6, 1962, pp. 6 f.
Schreiner rejects both the passive and the reflexive sense and maintains that the
Niphal form ought to be rendered by '(für) sich Segen erwerben, sich Segen ver-
schaffen', which seems a little strained. The purport of the passage is in all essentials
the same with this interpretation as with Procksch's.
[36] 'Das Kerygma des Jahwisten', *EvTh* 24, 1964, pp. 80 ff. (=*Gesammelte Studien
zum Alten Testament* (ThB 22), München 1964, pp. 351 ff.). Wolff here adopts
Schreiner's view of the sense of the Niphal form and agrees with Procksch in a
markedly universalistic interpretation.

בְּךָ יְבָרֵךְ יִשְׂרָאֵל לֵאמֹר   By you Israel shall bless, saying,

יְשִׂמְךָ אֱלֹהִים כְּאֶפְרַיִם   'God make you as Ephraim and

וְכִמְנַשֶּׁה   as Manasseh'.[37]

The meaning of 12.3 would then simply be that all nations will mention Abraham's name when pronouncing a blessing, wishing themselves just as overflowing a blessing as he received from God.

Unfortunately the Niphal form of ברך occurs, apart from this passage, only in Gen. 18.18 and 28.14, and both these passages are a reiteration of the promise to Abraham: thus the form is never found in a different context which might throw new light on the question of its meaning. But it appears to be an important argument that the Hithpael form of the same verb is found in precisely the same context. The promise to Abraham and to his seed is repeated several times in Genesis, and when it is quoted in Gen. 22.18 and 26.4, the Hithpael form is used: והתברכו בזרעך כל גויי הארץ. And in this case the rendering 'shall be blessed' is impossible; we must translate 'and in your seed all the nations of the earth shall bless themselves'.[38] It is difficult to believe that the grammatical variations in the formulations of the divine promise to the patriarchs should involve a difference also in content: clearly the same thing is meant when the promise is repeated in a slightly different form. Now the sense of the Hithpael is evident: thus the disputed Niphal can be made clear from the meaning of this form.[39] It may be added that there are in fact several passages in the Old Testament where the passive sense is manifest (e.g. Ps. 128.4), but in all these cases the Pual form is employed. From a grammatical point of view there can hardly be any doubt that the translation 'bless themselves' is to be preferred, as has been recognized by scholars like the elder Delitzsch,[40] Gunkel,[41] and Skinner.[42] It is also the rendering given in BDB and KBL s. v. ברך.

In fact to render Gen. 12.3b by 'in you all the families of the earth shall be blessed' is to read too much into it—behind such an inter-

---

[37] Cf. also Ruth 4.11 f. For further examples see Gunkel, *Genesis,* on 12.3.

[38] For ברך Hithp. 'bless oneself' see e.g. Ps. 72.17: note the parallelism יתברכו בו and יאשרוהו.

[39] Wolff, op. cit., p. 81, n. 31 (=p. 352, n. 31) admits that there is no difference in meaning between Gen. 12.3 and 22.18, 26.4, but maintains that the sense which he suggests for the Niph. must then be supposed to be valid also for the Hithp. This is surely an error of method: the sense of the disputed Niph. must of course be explained from the Hithp., of which the meaning is certain, not conversely!

[40] Franz Delitzsch, *Neuer Commentar über die Genesis,* Leipzig 1887, ad loc.

[41] *Genesis,* ad loc.

[42] J. Skinner, *A Critical and Exegetical Commentary on Genesis* (ICC), Edinburgh 1910, ad loc.

pretation lies ultimately the New Testament use of this passage in Acts 3.25 and Gal. 3.8, where Luke and Paul, following LXX, have rendered נברכו by ἐνευλογηθήσονται. We must take Gen. 12.3 as a statement about the abundance of the blessing which had been allotted to Abraham, not as an intimation of the final goal of a divine plan for the salvation of the world. Thus interpreted the passage admittedly becomes less charged with theological profundity, but this seems in fact more justified in view of the context: so advanced a universalism as the rendering by a passive form implies would be rather surprising in this connexion, lacking as it does real parallels in the work of the Yahwist. Gunkel[43] is doubtless right when he maintains that the narrator does not refer to something still in the future at the time of writing: the Yahwist had seen the promise of abundant blessing fulfilled in Israel's position as a great power under David and Solomon, when Abraham's seed was multitudinous and in possession of the land that Yhwh had once promised to the fathers. On this interpretation it becomes impossible to speak of a divine plan in J which embraces all history and which aims at the salvation of the whole world through the elect people. We must be content to recognize a shorter perspective: at a summit of Israelite prosperity the Yahwist looks back and sees the past as a series of purposeful divine actions, where even the corruption and disobedience of men have been forced to serve God's aims. This is true also of the separate stages of the way which the Yahwist surveys: the words of Joseph to his brothers in Gen. 45.5[44] are characteristic:

ועתה אל־תעצבו ואל־יחר	And now do not be distressed nor
בעיניכם כי־מכרתם אתי הנה	angry with yourselves because
כי למחיה שלחני אלהים לפניכם:	you sold me here; for to preserve life God sent me before you.

The Yahwist recognizes, in the words of E. A. Speiser, 'that a higher order and purpose may lie behind seemingly incomprehensible human events.'[45] This conviction is expressed above all in terms of divine promises which have been fulfilled in the course of history; the narrator does not use the concept of a fixed plan to express his understanding of Israel's past. The same view of history as a sequence of events in which

---

[43] Loc. cit.

[44] Here attributed to one stratum (J) with, e.g., Eissfeldt, *Hexateuch-Synopse*, pp. 92* f.; Speiser, *Genesis. Introduction, Translation, and Notes* (AB 1), Garden City, N.Y., 1964, pp. 340 f., against, e.g., Gunkel, *Genesis*, ad loc.; Noth, *Überlieferungsgeschichte des Pentateuch*, pp. 31; 38, who regard v. 5a as J and v. 5b as E. This dissection of the verse into two different sources seems to belong to the exaggerated niceties of literary criticism.

[45] *Genesis*, p. XXVII.

the purposes of God are in the end fulfilled emerges in the well-known words in Gen. 50.20, traditionally attributed to the Elohistic stratum:[46]

ואתם חשבתם עלי רעה אלהים	As for you, you meant evil against
חשבה לטבה למען עשה	me but God meant it for good,
כיום הזה להחית עם־רב:	to bring about what has now happened, to keep much people alive.

The Priestly source, too, expresses in some passages the view that a divine purpose is active in the course of events. A case in point is Ex. 29.46:[47]

וידעו כי אני יהוה אלהיהם אשר	And they shall know that I am
הוצאתי אתם מארץ מצרים לשכני	Yhwh their God, who brought
בתוכם	them forth out of the land of Egypt that I might dwell among them.

The goal of the events is here naturally conceived in a different way: the emphasis is not, as in J, on the fulfilment of the promises of land and progeny to the patriarchs but on God's holy presence in the cult instituted on Mount Sinai.[48]

The Deuteronomic History, as is well known, resembles the work of the Yahwist in an important respect: it is also written from what I called 'the viewpoint of a result already arrived at'. If the Yahwist surveys the distance covered from a height of Israelite history, the Deuteronomist looks back from a deep valley: he describes the downward path, towards the fall of Jerusalem, the deportations and the humiliations. He too sees the work of God in the events of history, but with him it is still more doubtful if we are really justified in speaking of a divine *plan* for the events. Lindblom[49] has made a distinction between two different ways of looking at history in Israel: the teleological and the dogmatic, and he maintains, no doubt rightly, that the teleological view is characteristic of J, whereas in the Deuteronomist's work the dogmatic aspect

---

[46] Cf. e.g. Eissfeldt, op. cit., p. 106*; Noth, op. cit., p. 38; Speiser, op. cit., pp. 374 f., 378.

[47] Generally ascribed to P: see e.g. Eissfeldt, op. cit., p. 153*; Noth, op cit., p. 18.

[48] 'Israel, in der Form der durch den עדה-Begriff charakterisierten Kultgemeinde, ist nach der Auffassung der Priesterschrift das Ziel der Wege Gottes mit der Menschheit.' (O. Plöger, *Theokratie und Eschatologie* (WMANT 2), Neukirchen 1959, p. 44).

[49] 'Historieskrivningen i Israel och dess ställning inom forntidens hävdateckning', *STK* 11, 1935, pp. 222 ff.

is predominant, i.e. the view that history is the realization of the law of retribution. The Deuteronomist regards the whole history of Israel as an illustration of this law: obedience to Yhwh's commandments brings blessing, apostasy leads to judgment. But Lindblom finds the teleological view too in the Deuteronomic History. He does not adduce any examples, but there are indubitably passages that express the idea of a purpose, a divine intention in history. One could think of the Nathan oracle in 2 Sam. 7, which clearly speaks of a future goal (v. 10):

<table>
<tr><td dir="rtl">ושמתי מקום לעמי לישראל
ונטעתיו ושכן תחתיו ולא ירגז
עוד ולא־יסיפו בני־עולה
לענותו כאשר בראשונה:</td><td>I will appoint a place for my people Israel and I will plant it that it may dwell in its own place, and be disturbed no more, and wicked men shall afflict them no more, as formerly.</td></tr>
</table>

And of the Davidic scion it is said (v. 13):

<table>
<tr><td dir="rtl">כנתי את־כסא ממלכתו עד־עולם:</td><td>I will establish the throne of his kingdom for ever.</td></tr>
</table>

If one wants to call this too a divine plan in history, the word 'plan' must certainly be used in a very weakened sense: it is a matter of a divine purpose which aims at securing for Israel a safe position among the nations and at maintaining the Davidic dynasty, and this purpose is revealed in the word of the prophet. The author of this theology of history is above all concerned with what von Rad calls 'das Problem des Funktionierens des Wortes Jahwes in der Geschichte',[50] as for instance in the story of Rehoboam's unsuccessful negotiations with the people in Shechem (1 Kings 12.15):

<table>
<tr><td dir="rtl">ולא־שמע המלך אל־העם כי־
היתה סבה מעם יהוה למען
הקים את־דברו אשר דבר יהוה
ביד אחיה השילני אל־ירבעם
בן־נבט:</td><td>So the king did not listen to the people; for it was a turn of affairs from Yhwh that he might fulfil his word which Yhwh spoke by Ahijah the Shilonite to Jeroboam the son of Nebat.</td></tr>
</table>

Statements of this kind recur time and again in the Deuteronomist's work,[51] and form as it were a pattern in the web of events. God speaks through a prophet, and his word is fulfilled in what happens; it creates

---

[50] *Theologie des AT* I, p. 341. Cf. above p. 64.
[51] Cf. von Rad, *Deuteronomiumstudien*, pp. 54 ff. (=*Gesammelte Studien*, pp. 192 ff.), and *Theologie des AT* I, pp. 338 ff.

history, but in a twofold way: for judgment or for deliverance.[52] It appears more justifiable to regard this pattern as characteristic of the Deuteronomic view of history than to stress the idea of a plan: there may possibly be certain traces of such an idea, but it is never expressly formulated nor consistently carried through.

It is generally admitted that the scheme of retribution is still more rigorously applied in the Chronicler's account of history. Here too the prophecy of Nathan (1 Chr. 17) is employed to suggest the forward perspective, that hope of a future according to the divine promise which the Chronicler appears to have shared.[53] His central concern, however, the principal aim of his comprehensive survey of past history from Adam onwards, seem to be to legitimate existing institutions, to represent the post-exilic community in Jerusalem as the true heir of the ancient Israel and the perfect realization of the ideal of theocracy.[54] Thus once more it is a matter of writing history from the aspect of the attained result. The fact that the perspective is so long implies, however, only seemingly an understanding of history as one coherent whole. As the Chronicler applies the principle of retribution to each single generation, the sense of the history of Israel as a unity is weakened: it threatens to resolve into a number of isolated sections.[55] Already here we seem to have the origin of the view of history peculiar to the rabbinic literature, where history is not understood as a unity but disintegrates into individual episodes and situations; a *heilsgeschichtlich* perspective is entirely lacking.[56] But in so far as the Chronicler is unable to understand the sequence of events as a unity, it becomes more difficult to speak about a divine plan in history in any strict sense of the word. The messianic hope which appears to emerge may suggest certain ideas of Yhwh's future aims, and of course the Chronicler knows of purpose-

---

[52] von Rad, *Theologie des AT* I, p. 341.

[53] Cf. Noth, *Überlieferungsgeschichtliche Studien. Die sammelnden und bearbeitenden Geschichtswerke im Alten Testament*, 2. Aufl., Tübingen 1957, p. 179. On the Chronicler's concern for the dynastic principle and his hope for the restoration of the kingdom with a descendant of David on the throne see also the brief but suggestive paper by D. N. Freedman, 'The Chronicler's Purpose', CBQ 23, 1961, pp. 436 ff. Cf. also von Rad, op. cit., pp. 347 f.

[54] Strongly emphasized by W. Rudolph, *Chronikbücher* (HAT I: 21), Tübingen 1955, pp. XXII f., as also by Plöger, op. cit., pp. 50 ff. Cf. also Noth, op cit., pp. 174 ff.; Freedman, op. cit., pp. 436 ff.

[55] Emphasized by von Rad, op. cit., pp. 346 f.

[56] D. Rössler, *Gesetz und Geschichte. Untersuchungen zur Theologie der jüdischen Apokalyptik und der pharisäischen Orthodoxie* (WMANT 3), 2. Aufl., Neukirchen 1962, pp. 24; 29; 40 ff.

ful divine acts in Israel's past history, but that seems to be the closest he comes to the concept of a plan in what happens.

The examination of the Hebrew terms for a 'plan' in history showed that most of the comparatively few instances could be found in the prophetic literature. The question is whether there are in the prophets further passages which testify to the idea of a divine plan in history without the very term being used.

Generally speaking the prophets do of course, by constantly announcing an imminent divine action in judgment or salvation, proclaim God's purposes, what he intends to do. It is superfluous to quote any examples from the abundant and well-known material. But the message that Yhwh intends to act in the near future to punish or to save Israel cannot be said to imply the idea of a 'plan in history', except if the term is again used in a rather diluted sense.

In Deutero-Isaiah the prediction of the future plays an important rôle as evidence of Yhwh's divine power, as for instance in 44.8:[57]

אל־תפחדו ואל־תרהו הלא מאז	Fear not, do not be terrified;[58]
השמעתיך והגדתי ואתם עדי	did I not tell you and declare it
היש אלוה מבלעדי ואין צור	long ago? And you are my
בל־ידעתי:	witnesses. Is there a god besides me? There is no Rock; I know not any.

The presupposition for Deutero-Isaiah's whole argument is that Yhwh has decided in advance what is going to happen and has revealed his intentions to his messengers[59] in accordance with the famous words in the Book of Amos (3.7):

כי לא יעשה אדני יהוה דבר	For the Lord Yhwh does nothing
כי אם־גלה סודו אל־עבדיו	without revealing his secret to
הנביאים:	his servants the prophets.

The word סוד means 'intimate circle, confidential speech, secret counsel'; here it clearly denotes Yhwh's hidden decisions and purposes, which he discloses to the prophets. There is no talk of a fixed plan in any strict sense. That it is Yhwh who decrees what is going to occur is

[57] Cf. also 41.26; 43.9 ff.; 45.21.

[58] Cf. KBL sub ירה.

[59] 'Yahweh alone is God: he is God because in times past he predicted events which have now happened, God because he is ready now with announcements of "new things" still to come. And the reason why he, and he alone, knows the future, is that he in fact controls history.' (C. R. North, *The Second Isaiah. Introduction, Translation and Commentary to Chapters XL–LV*, Oxford 1964, p. 16).

a statement which is found in many variations in different prophets. Jer. 4.27 f. is a characteristic example:

כי־כה אמר יהוה שממה תהיה
כל־הארץ וכלה לא אעשה:
על־זאת תאבל הארץ וקדרו
השמים ממעל על כי־דברתי זמתי
ולא נחמתי ולא־אשוב ממנה:

For thus says Yhwh: 'The whole land shall be a desolation, though I will not make a full end. For this the earth shall mourn, and the heavens above be black. For I have spoken and not relented, I have decided and will not turn back.[60]

Again in Isa. 37.26 (cf. 2 Kings 19.25) Sennacherib is reminded that he is allowed to ravage only with the sanction of Yhwh, who controls the course of events:

הלוא־שמעת למרחוק אותה
עשיתי מימי קדם ויצרתיה עתה
הבאתיה ותהי להשאות גלים
נצים ערים בצרות:

Have you not heard that I prepared (lit., did) it long ago? From days of old I formed it: now I bring it to pass, that you should lay waste fortified cities into heaps of ruins.

Yhwh's power to determine what happens in history is sometimes expressed in the same way as in the Deuteronomic History: the prophets speak of a divine word which is fulfilled in the historical events, as for instance in Ez. 12.25:

כי אני יהוה אדבר את אשר
אדבר דבר ויעשה לא תמשך
עוד כי בימיכם בית המרי
אדבר דבר ועשיתיו נאם אדני
יהוה:

For I, Yhwh, will speak. The word that I shall speak shall come to pass.[61] It shall no longer be delayed, for in your days, O rebellious house, will I speak a word and perform it, says the Lord Yhwh.

This is the view of history which is programmatically epitomized in Lam. 2.17:[62]

---

[60] The verbs in the last sentence have been transposed with LXX, BH³ and most commentaries. זמם means literally 'purpose, devise', but the translation 'decide' here is justified in the context: cf. Rudolph's 'ich habs beschlossen' (*Jeremia*, ad loc.).

[61] For this translation of this syntactically difficult sentence see the detailed analysis by W. Zimmerli, *Ezechiel* (BKAT XIII), Neukirchen [1955 ff.], ad loc.

[62] Cf. my *Studies in the Text and Theology of the Book of Lamentations. With a Critical Edition of the Peshitta Text* (Studia Theologica Lundensia 21), Lund 1963, pp. 236 f.

עשה יהוה אשר זמם	Yhwh has done what he had devised,
בצע אמרתו	he has fulfilled his word;
אשר צוה מימי־קדם	as he decreed long ago,
הרס ולא חמל	he has demolished without pity.

I do not think it is possible to get much further in the prophetic material. Once more we must conclude, as we did with regard to the passages where the word 'plan' itself was used about the acts of God in history, that the idea of a definite divine purpose in events is clearly found in the Old Testament prophets, as is also the conception that Yhwh reveals his aims and announces his decisions, but that it is not possible to speak of a plan in any strict sense of the word. It is hardly a coincidence that Fichtner, after having asserted rather categorically that Yhwh's plan in history is an important *motif* in Isaiah's message, is then forced to make vital qualifications and reservations.[63] He admits that we are never told of any details or individual elements of this plan: Isaiah knows that he has been informed about Yhwh's decree, and this knowledge he works out 'in verschiedenen Linien . . ., die sich zum Teil überkreuzen und doch alle auf dasselbe Ziel hinführen'.[64] What remains, then, is the general idea of Yhwh's purposeful acts in history.[65]

It may be well to make here a distinction which has been implicit in some of what has been said above but which ought perhaps to be explicitly put into words. In the expression 'the divine plan in history', *history* is an ambiguous word and may mean two rather different things. It may refer to a limited series of events, an episode or an epoch; or it may denote all history, the entire succession of events from creation to consummation, that which is sometimes called universal history (*Universalgeschichte*). Now there is of course a great difference between a plan in a limited sequence of occurrences and a plan in History with capital H: the view that Yhwh acts purposefully in what happens is not necessarily identical with the idea that history as a whole is heading for a definite goal along a road laid out according to a fixed plan. I am afraid these two concepts have not always been properly distinguished. In the Old Testament we mostly meet the first: in so far as it is at all possible to speak of a plan it concerns a definite chain of events and a limited goal. As we have seen, the Yahwist regards the historical development up to the conquest and the establishment of the state as

---

[63] 'Jahves Plan in der Botschaft des Jesaja', *ZAW* 63 (N.F. 22), 1951, pp. 27; 32.
[64] Op. cit., p. 32.
[65] Cf. also the criticisms of Fichtner in an important article by G. Fohrer, 'Prophetie und Geschichte', *ThLZ* 89, 1964, col. 497.

a series of purposeful divine acts, but his perspective does not include all that happens; it cannot possibly be said to embrace the course of history in its entirety.[66] This is naturally true of all accounts which look back from a definite point in history on the way which Israel had travelled and trace Yhwh's will and aims in what has happened. These chains of events and these goals may be different in different texts, and so it is difficult to speak of one and the same divine plan in all passages. It is perhaps possible to find a common denominator in the different divine plans, but hardly one uniform divine plan.

If we look for the universal perspective, the idea of a divine plan in history as a totality, the relevant texts are fewer still. When we glimpse a goal for all history in the eschatological sayings of the prophets, there hardly appears such a survey of past events as could possibly justify any talk of a divine plan for history as a whole;[66a] and both the universalistic views of future and the particularistic prophecies of bliss reveal rather a divine purpose than a plan in any strict sense.

Properly speaking it is only in one place that we can find the idea of a divine plan in history and speak of such a plan without considerable reservations: in the apocalyptic literature. In the Book of Daniel we meet a clear and schematic idea of the course of world history, where successive kingdoms supersede one another in a development which is ultimately not controlled by the actions of earthly rulers but is determined by God according to his will, and the details of this divinely planned development, above all those stages of it which lie still in the future, are revealed to the apocalyptist. Though the actual word 'plan' is never used about the divine control of history in Daniel, the idea is clearly there—much more so than in any other Old Testament writing. Admittedly the perspective of the author of the Book of Daniel does not in fact embrace the whole of world history, conceived as a unity from beginning to end: the visions and the revelations strictly speaking concern only a portion of universal history.[67] Nevertheless it appears

---

[66] According to Lindblom, the Yahwist's perspective of history includes also the consummation of this age according to God's decision ('denna tidsålders fulländning efter Guds rådslut', STK 11, 1935, p. 223), but as far as I can see there is no real foundation for this in J.

[66a] Cf. A. Alt, 'Die Deutung der Weltgeschichte im Alten Testament', ZThK 56, 1959, p. 137.

[67] Cf. O. Plöger's comment on Dan. 2: '... so könnte man Kap. 2 eine sachliche Einführung nennen, die uns an die Frage nach der Geschichte und ihrem Ende heranführt, der der Verfasser des Danielbuches entscheidende Bedeutung beilegt. Aber diese Geschichte, dargestellt an den vier Reichen, die jedoch eine schicksalhafte Einheit bilden, und das Ende ihrer Geschichte umfassen nun nicht wie in der alten Vorstellung von den Weltperioden die gesamte Weltgeschichte von ihren Anfängen bis

justifiable to speak here of the idea of a divine plan. It is not, as in the prophets, merely the purpose of Yhwh which is proclaimed: we are shown a detailed picture of a development in history governed by God, a picture which indicates also the individual stages of the way towards the ultimate goal. The course of future history is foretold and presented in a carefully calculated time scheme; the whole sequence of events is represented as determined in detail beforehand. This well-known difference between prophecy and apocalyptic[68] may perhaps also be expressed thus: the prophets know of a divine purpose in history, the apocalyptists of a fixed plan.

The conclusion appears inevitable: the phrase 'the divine plan in history' is hardly suitable when we want to define what is typical of the Old Testament view of history as a whole. Even when words which may be translated 'plan' are used, they do not denote a detailed scheme, and it is entirely impossible to speak of *the* divine plan in history, as different Old Testament authors describe different 'plans', which are executed in various limited sequences of events. It is evident that we ought to use less precise terms: Yhwh pursues certain aims, a divine purpose is discernible in all that happens.

But if this is so, then the question of the distinctiveness of the Old Testament view appears in a somewhat different light. It is true that the gods of the neighbouring peoples are often represented as aimless, fitful, and arbitrary, acting without purpose: typical of the current simplification is the way in which Yhwh is contrasted against the other gods in the following description: 'It was not, in fact, primarily in the

---

zur Gegenwart des Verfassers; es ist vielmehr ein historisch überschaubarer Abschnitt aus dieser Geschichte, der in dem Zeitpunkt beginnt, in dem Israel als selbständiges Volk aus der Geschichte ausscheidet, also gleichsam eine Weltgeschichte ohne Israel.' (*Das Buch Daniel* (KAT XVIII), Gütersloh 1965, p. 56). K. Koch's characterization of the Book of Daniel as 'ein universalgeschichtlicher Entwurf' ('Spätisraelitisches Geschichtsdenken am Beispiel des Buches Daniel', *HZ* 193, 1961, p. 31) is thus hardly justified.

[68] Cf. for instance P. Volz, *Die Eschatologie der jüdischen Gemeinde im neutestamentlichen Zeitalter nach den Quellen der rabbinischen, apokalyptischen und apokryphen Literatur,* Tübingen 1934, p. 6: 'Was die Propheten einst über den Untergang Israels hinübertrug: der Glaube, dass er von Jahwe komme, das ist hier in viel weiterer, freilich nicht selten kleinlicherer Ausgestaltung ausgesponnen. Nicht der Feind, nicht der Zufall regiert, Gott hat seinen Lieblingen, den alten Vätern, alles schon vorausgesagt; in himmlischen Büchern, auf himmlischen Tafeln ist es von Urzeit her eingetragen. Und mit dem geistigen Blick, der in die Tiefen des göttlichen Plans eindringt, weiss der Apokalyptiker, der Geheimwisser, warum alles so kommen musste, welchen Zweck und welche Stelle das einzelne Ereignis im Geschichtsplan Gottes hat.'

repeatable events of nature, but in unrepeatable historical events, that Yahweh manifested himself; and in these events, unlike the pagan gods, he acted purposively.'[69] But the statement that the gods of Israel's neighbours were not believed to be capable of purposeful actions in history is manifestly misleading, as even a cursory glance at the texts will show. Several of the quotations from extra-biblical sources adduced above in the previous chapters not only testify to ideas of historical events as divine actions but also represent these actions as purposive. In the Sumerian composition called 'The Curse of Akkad', Enlil is represented as bringing the Gutians down from their mountains to ravage Akkad—not arbitrarily, because of a divine whim, but with the clear purpose of avenging his sanctuary in Nippur, which had been destroyed by Naramsin, the ruler of Akkad. And so of course all texts which represent historical disasters as divine punishment for sacrilege and sin in fact presuppose that the gods act purposively in history. The Era Epic ends with a kind of 'oracle of bliss':[70] the god Era decrees the restoration of the ravaged country and promises the oppressed people a glorious triumph over the hated enemies; the insignificant remnant shall again become a mighty people to which the inhabitants of all countries will bring their tribute. Though the whole context is naturally different in many respects, it is impossible to deny the striking similarities with Old Testament prophecies of restoration, not least in the idea of a divinely decreed future of unclouded prosperity.[71] If we are entitled to speak of a divine 'plan' in history in the Israelite oracles of salvation, the same must be true here: the prophecy outlines the divine purpose in the future of the elect people.[72] Again, the texts which describe the divine appointment of kings often mention that they have been chosen to carry out an explicit purpose of the deity, as for instance the Sumerian ruler Nur-Adad, who is commissioned to execute the god Utu's intention to recapture and restore Larsa.[73] Similarly 'the great lord

---

[69] J. Bright, 'Hebrew Religion, History of', in *The Interpreter's Dictionary of the Bible . . .*, 2, New York–Nashville 1962, p. 562.

[70] Cf. above, p. 32, and see Lambert's edition of 'The Fifth Tablet of the Era Epic' in *Iraq* 24, 1962, pp. 119 ff., especially ll. 25–37, pp. 122 f.

[71] Cf. Gössmann, *Das Era-Epos*, pp. 83 f.

[72] Cf. Ebeling's summing up of the tendency of the epic: 'Der Mythos *šar gimir dadmê* [i.e. the Era Epic] hat eine bestimmte politische Situation als Thema, bei der Babylon in grosse Not geraten ist. Die Dichtung zeigt, dass es trotz der Heimsuchungen aus einem kleinen Rest wieder dank göttlicher Fügung zu einem grossen Volke werden muss.' (*Bruchstücke eines politischen Propagandagedichtes aus einer assyrischen Kanzlei* (MAOG 12: 2), Leipzig 1938, p. 2, n. 1.)

[73] Cf. above, p. 48.

Marduk entrusted the righteous sceptre' to Nabu-apla-iddina in order that the god's purposes should be carried out.[74]

The inscriptions of Esarhaddon, king of Assyria, contain among other things a detailed report of how he rebuilt Babylon, which had been destroyed by his father Sennacherib, whom he succeeded in 680 B.C. He describes first how the inhabitants of Babylon plundered Esagila, Marduk's famous shrine in the city, in order to get means to pay the Elamites for assistance in a rebellion against Assyria. This sacrilege excited the god's wrath:[75]

i-gu-ug-ma ^d*en-líl ilâni*^{meš} ^d*marduk*	The Enlil ('Lord') of the gods,
a-na sa-pan mâti ḫul-lu-qu	Marduk, became angry. To over-
nišê^{meš}*-šá ik-ta-pu-ud*	throw the country, to destroy
lemuttim (HUL-*tim*)	its people he planned evil.

And we are further told how this divine plan was carried out:[76]

nišê^{meš}*a-šib qer-bé-(e-)šu a-na*	The people living in its midst
ṣi-in-di ù bir-te zu-'-ú-zu il-li-ku	were apportioned to bonds and
re-e-šu-tú 70 šánâti^{meš} *mi-nu-ut*	fetters and went into slavery.
ni-du-ti-šu iš-ṭur-ma re-me-nu-ú	Seventy years as the measure of
^d*marduk sur-riš lìb-ba-šu i-nu-*	its desolation he wrote. But the
uḫ-ma e-liš a-na šap-liš uš-bal-kit-	merciful Marduk, whose heart
ma a-na 11 šánâti^{meš} *a-šab-šú iq-bi*	calmed down instantaneously,
	reversed (the figures) and ordered
	its restoration in the eleventh
	year.

The text is interesting from several points of view. The verb 'to plan' (*kapādu*) is used about Marduk to describe his evil devices against the impious population of Babylon. This plan includes among other things an exile lasting seventy years—the parallel with Jer. 25.11 f.; 29.10 needs hardly to be pointed out. The god's deeds in history are thus represented as a purposeful activity, though the future course of events is not inexorably laid down according to a fixed and detailed plan but rather dependant upon the general purpose of the deity, which admits

---

[74] Cf. above, pp. 48 f.

[75] Borger, *Die Inschriften Asarhaddons*, p. 13 (Bab. A–G, Episode 5 a). An English translation of the accounts of the restoration of Babylon is found in Luckenbill, *Ancient Records of Assyria and Babylonia*, II, pp. 242 ff.

[76] Borger, op. cit., p. 15 (Bab. A–G, Episode 9 c, 10 a).

a certain flexibility[77]—much as in the Hebrew prophets, who sometimes describe the impending judgment as conditional or alterable, depending on the people's conversion and Yhwh's mercy.

A kind of divine plan for the course of history seems also to be implied in the well-known ideas of the tablets of destiny, *tup-šimāti,* and the fixing of destinies.[78] To determine the fates is a divine privilege, and the tablets of destiny are a symbol of this power. Little is known of them: they figure in some myths, but we are never told their origin or any other details about them. In the Epic of Creation Marduk (or originally Enlil) defeats Kingu, the second spouse of Tiamat, and takes from him the tablets of destiny, which had been given to him by Tiamat. Marduk then fastens them on his own breast as a token of the supreme authority which he had been promised by the gods in assembly if he could save them from the rebel monsters. In another myth the bird-god Zû (or, according to a recent suggestion, Anzû)[79] contrives to steal the tablets of destiny from Enlil, whose control of the universe is thereby threatened. A saviour has to be found to defeat the usurper and recapture the tablets (the rôle of the hero is played by different gods in different versions of the story). It is at least clear that the possession of the tablets signifies the supreme power over gods and men. That this power is attributed to several members of the Mesopotamian pantheon is perhaps not so surprising: we must not expect logical consistency in the ancient myths. Some passages even give the impression that the fixing of the destinies did not belong to one god alone but to the whole assembly of gods.[80] There is also some ambiguity as to the time for which the destinies were determined: it is sometimes stated that this

---

[77] The expression 'reversed (the figures)' is due to the fact that the cuneiform sign for 70 becomes 11 if the two elements of the sign are reversed: 70 is written 𐏓, 11 is written ⟨𐏓. Luckenbill (op. cit., p. 242) compares our 9, which becomes 6 if it is turned upside down. A closer parallel, however, would be our 71, which is reduced to 17 when the figures are reversed.

[78] For the Mesopotamian ideas of destiny, and especially the 'tablets of destiny' see C. Fichtner–Jeremias, *Der Schicksalsglaube bei den Babyloniern* (MVAG 27: 2), Leipzig 1922, esp. pp. 20 ff.; Meissner, *Babylonien und Assyrien* II, pp. 124 ff.; M. David, *Les dieux et le Destin en Babylonie,* Paris 1949, esp. pp. 89 ff.; F. Nötscher, 'Schicksalsglaube in Qumrân und Umwelt', *BZ* N.F. 3, 1959, pp. 205 ff. (the first part of this article is an excellent survey of the Babylonian and Assyrian ideas of destiny); Oppenheim, *Ancient Mesopotamia,* pp. 201 ff.

[79] So B. Landsberger, 'Einige unerkannt gebliebene oder verkannte Nomina des Akkadischen', *WZKM* 57, 1961, pp. 1 ff.

[80] In this form the belief seems to have been current among the Hittites too: cf. Gurney, 'Hittite kingship', *Myth, Ritual, and Kingship,* p. 108.

was done 'for eternity',[80a] but at the same time the fixing of the fates is a yearly ceremony (as for instance at the New Year Festival in Babylon). Perhaps the ancients did not feel any inconsistency here.[81]

Whatever uncertainties there may be in details it is at any rate evident that the conception of a divine fixing of the destinies implies the belief that the gods or the supreme god determine beforehand the future sequence of events. Undeniably this comes fairly close to the idea of a divine plan for the course of history, though the deterministic aspect is perhaps more pronounced than the teleological. The same conceptions seem to lie behind the use of the terms $e/isurtu$ and $usurtu$, 'which means drawing or plan, design, apparently referring to some kind of divinely predetermined—outlined, even "blueprinted"—course of events that determines all happenings'.[82] Enlil is for instance called $mu\text{-}sir$ $e\text{-}su\text{-}rat$ $šamê$ u $ersetim$, 'who draws the plans for heaven and earth'.[83] These ideas go back to Sumerian theologians who believed that the cosmos was 'controlled in accordance with the well-laid plans and duly prescribed laws of a divine pantheon'.[84] One is almost tempted to say that in certain respects we are more justified in speaking of a fixed divine plan for history in Mesopotamian religion than in the Old Testament. Exception should possibly be made for the Book of Daniel; but then it is not improbable that there is a connexion between the apocalyptists' idea of a fixed plan for history and the Babylonian belief in the unchangeable decrees of the gods.[85]

The idea of a divine plan and a purposeful action in history is often said to be connected with a particular view of the course of events as a linear development, which is contrasted with a cyclic view. Mowinckel for instance describes the difference between the Israelite view of history and that of other ancient peoples in the following manner: 'All

---

[80a] See e.g. the building inscription 'Nebukadnezar Nr. 15', Langdon–Zehnpfund, *Die neubabylonischen Königsinschriften*, p. 126, col. II, l. 63. Cf. Fichtner–Jeremias, op. cit., p. 34.

[81] Cf. the Enthronement psalms in the Old Testament: it is affirmed yearly that 'Yhwh has become king' but this statement does not, of course, imply that he does not reign from all eternity.

[82] Oppenheim, *Ancient Mesopotamia*, p. 204.

[83] Tallqvist, *Akkadische Götterepitheta*, p. 104 (with further examples).

[84] Kramer, 'Sumerian Historiography', *IEJ* 3, 1953, p. 219.

[85] Cf. R. Eppel, 'Les tables de la Loi et les tables célestes', *RHPR* 17, 1937, p. 407: 'Là encore ils [i.e. the apocalyptists] ont pu s'appuyer sur une idée fondamentale de la religion assyro-babylonienne, celle que non seulement les choses, mais aussi les événements historiques, aussi les destins des hommes préexistent dans le ciel, qu'ils y sont écrits. Le drame historique et cosmique se déroule suivant des décrets immuables des dieux, arrêtés à l'avance et inscrits sur des tables comme des lois.'

the ancient religions and civilizations, even those of Greece, conceived of the course of history as a circle, corresponding to the annual cycle of the life of nature. The Old Testament conceives of history as a straight line, pointing to a goal'.[86] The Babylonians in particular are often said to have held a cyclic view of history.[87] This appears to contradict what has just been said about the similarities of the Israelite and the Mesopotamian ideas, which would be almost inexplicable if there were such a radical divergence in the basic conceptions of history. On closer inspection, however, the statements about the alleged cyclic view of history in Mesopotamia appear to be both vague and lacking support in the Akkadian texts. The expression seems to be used in at least three different senses. Sometimes the idea has been linked up with the Babylonian New Year Festival as a ritual reenactment of the primeval drama:[88] in that case the 'circle' is a yearly cycle. Sometimes it is stressed that certain chronicles tend to represent the course of history as alternating periods of prosperity and disaster,[89] and it is concluded that the ancient historians saw 'the past in terms of recurring cycles'.[90] Again, a third interpretation of the alleged cyclic view concerns a much larger perspective and implies an endless repetition of the whole temporal process

---

[86] *He That Cometh*, Oxford 1956, p. 151. Cf. the similar statement by M. Burrows: 'Through all the ancient Israelite interpretations of history runs a consistent and characteristic understanding of time as proceeding in a straight line, with a beginning and an end. This is in sharp and obvious contrast with the ideas of history prevalent among many other peoples as consisting of an endless recurrence of cycles leading nowhere.' ('Ancient Israel', *The Idea of History in the Ancient Near East*, ed. Dentan, p. 127). For an illuminating discussion and some sound criticisms of the alleged contrast between the cyclic view of the Greeks and the Hebrew view of time as a straight line see J. Barr, *Biblical Words for Time* (SBT 33), London 1962, pp. 137 ff.

[87] Cf. e.g. the following statement: 'That the Babylonians did regard history as cyclical is well attested by historical omens.' (A. K. Grayson–W. G. Lambert, 'Akkadian Prophecies', *JCS* 18, 1964, p. 10). The foundation for this assertion is however not very strong; the text continues: 'These presume that whenever a certain natural phenomenon occurs, there will always be a certain concomitant historical event. The same natural phenomenon is always (in theory) accompanied by the same historical event.' Surely the idea of a regular connexion between a certain portent and a certain event is not in itself equivalent to a cyclic view of history? Cf. the definition below, p. 95.

[88] E.g. by M. Eliade, *Le mythe de l'éternel retour*, Paris 1949, pp. 89 ff.

[89] Güterbock, 'Die historische Tradition und ihre literarische Gestaltung bei Babyloniern und Hethitern bis 1200', *ZA* 42 (N.F. 8), pp. 13 ff. ('die Geschichte als Wechsel von Heils- und Unheilszeiten', p. 13).

[90] Speiser, 'Ancient Mesopotamia', *The Idea of History in the Ancient Near East*, ed. Dentan, p. 56. Speiser speaks also of 'an almost rhythmic regularity of this unvarying alternation' (p. 55).

over a period of thousands of years.[91] The first of these conceptions does not really affect the understanding of historical events and so need not engage us more here.[92] That history is pictured as a succession of periods of bliss and adversity seems to be little more than a natural reflexion of the fact that prosperity and misfortunes actually did alternate in the history of Mesopotamian rulers and empires. What else could we expect? To call this a cyclic view seems to be a very loose use of the phrase; 'a cyclic view of history' must certainly be much more clearly defined. If we exchange 'temporal' for 'historical', Brandon's definition of the cyclic view of time should serve the purpose: it is a conception 'according to which the temporal process is regarded as moving in cycles, usually with a preconceived pattern, so that the same order of events perpetually repeats itself'.[93] On this reasonable definition Mesopotamian historiography is not evidence for a cyclic view.[94] Finally as regards the longer perspective the idea is entirely unknown in Akkadian texts and is found only in late accounts of the teaching of Berossos and similar sources.[95] We do not know to what extent this conception had been developed earlier.

Thus we may safely conclude that there is very little foundation for the not uncommon view that history was regarded as cyclic in Mesopotamia. G. Goossens speaks instead of 'une conception ondulatoire',[96] which seems a better expression, applicable both to the Mesopotamian view and to that of the Deuteronomist. There seems in fact to be no clear difference on this point between Israel and its neighbours, and so it is wholly consistent that they all know the idea of purposeful divine actions toward a definite goal in history.[97]

---

[91] See e.g. Meissner, *Babylonien und Assyrien*, II, pp. 117 f.

[92] For a detailed discussion and criticism of Eliade's interpretation of the Babylonian New Year ritual see S. G. F. Brandon, *History, Time and Deity. A Historical and Comparative Study of the Conception of Time in Religious Thought and Practice*, Manchester–New York 1965, pp. 71 ff.

[93] Op. cit., p. 4.

[94] Cf. also Gese, 'Geschichtliches Denken im Alten Orient und im Alten Testament', *ZThK* 55, 1958, pp. 127, 133 f.

[95] Meissner, loc. cit.; Brandon, op. cit., pp. 83 f.

[96] 'La philosophie de l'histoire dans l'Ancien Orient', *Sacra Pagina. Miscellanea biblica congressus internationalis catholici de re biblica*, Gembloux 1959, pp. 244 ff., and also in his review of *The Idea of History in the Ancient Near East*, ed. Dentan, in *BiOr* 13, 1956, pp. 189 ff.

[97] G. Östborn, *Yhwh's Words and Deeds. A Preliminary Study into the Old Testament Presentation of History* (UUA 1951: 7), Uppsala 1951, pp. 60 ff., attempts to demonstrate that the cyclic idea 'profoundly marked' the entire Old Testament, but his argument is neither clear nor convincing.

In this chapter I have attempted to show that the Old Testament does not speak so much of a divine 'plan' in a proper sense as is commonly assumed, and that the idea of the deity's purposeful control of history and of the belief in the course of events as a realization of divine intentions are common to the ancient Near East. It ought to be added that even so some differences seem to remain in this field, though they are perhaps mostly differences of degree. It goes without saying that the idea of a divine purpose in history must be rather differently conceived in a polytheistic religion and in the Old Testament.[98] Hebrew monotheism naturally does not allow of any ideas of rival plans and conflicting divine aims, but strongly enhances the tendency to a unitary perspective of history. But this is ultimately not so much a different understanding of history as a different conception of the deity; the basic difference concerns the idea of God and the possible difference in the view of the divine purpose in history is only a corollary. Perhaps it is also possible to assert that Old Testament historiography has sometimes a longer perspective and so a conception of a more distant aim for the divine activity, but this is certainly a difference in degree and not a basically different conception. And it ought not to be forgotten that there are instances of quite a long perspective in Akkadian texts too: the Yahwist's line from creation to the Solomonic empire has a parallel in the Babylonian Epic of Creation, which begins likewise with creation and culminates in the foundation of Babylon and its sanctuary Esagila. The differences between the two works are of course immense, but they seem to share the fundamental perspective of a purposeful development from the creation of the world up to an existing state of affairs in history.[99] Sometimes the Babylonian view—or certain aspects

---

[98] Cf. Speiser, 'The Biblical Idea of History in its Common Near Eastern Setting', *IEJ* 7, 1957, p. 203: 'The outstanding single feature of the cosmos of the ancient Mesopotamians was the tenet that no single god is the ultimate source of power and authority; none is truly omnipotent.' It must, however, be emphasized that this feature was to a certain extent neutralized by strong monotheistic tendencies: see J. Hehn, *Die biblische und die babylonische Gottesidee. Die israelitische Gottesauffassung im Lichte der altorientalischen Religionsgeschichte*, Leipzig 1913, pp. 96 ff.
[99] Cf. Noth's comment on the Babylonian Epic of Creation: 'So wird die Weltschöpfung selbst zur Einleitung einer Geschichte, die in der Weltmachtstellung des babylonischen Reiches ihren Zielpunkt hat.' ('Die Historisierung des Mythus im Alten Testament', *CuW* 4, 1928, p. 267). This transition from myth to history, common to J and *Enūma eliš*, has been denied by Weiser, who sees in the Babylonian text only the idea of an endless cyclic process (*Glaube und Geschichte* 1931, pp. 26 f.=1961, pp. 119 f.), but cf. Hempel, *Altes Testament und Geschichte*, pp. 12 f., and G. Widengren, 'Myth and History in Israelite-Jewish Thought', *Culture in History. Essays in Honor of Paul Radin*, New York 1960, pp. 484 f.

of it—should perhaps be defined as more deterministic than teleological, but then this difference cuts right through the Israelite material, dividing apocalyptists and prophets. And in those Hebrew authors who represent the teleological view, the *telos*, as we have seen, is conceived in rather diverging ways. There is no reason to attempt to make the Old Testament conceptions more unitary than they are, nor to exaggerate their difference from the neighbouring peoples. In this domain, as in so many others, the Old Testament faith is expressed in categories of thought common to the entire ancient Near East.

7 – 567-4054

CHAPTER SIX

Historical Events as Divine Revelation

The extra-biblical texts quoted in the foregoing pages have been evidence of a general ancient Near Eastern belief in divine acts in history and a purposeful guidance of the course of events, sometimes executed through the word of the deity. The current characterization of what is peculiarly Israelite stresses not only that Yhwh acts in history but also —and perhaps primarily—that Yhwh *reveals* himself in historical events; the emphasis is on history as a—or rather *the*—medium of revelation. As the difference between the Old Testament and the general Near Eastern views have so far turned out to be considerably less marked than is commonly thought, it seems worth while to continue the comparison on this point as well. Are there, in the extra-biblical material, any statements or passages which show that historical events were regarded not only as divine actions but also as divine revelation?

Perhaps a few words should be said here about the concept of revelation. I am using the word in a rather general and conventional sense, to mean everything whereby the deity gives men knowledge of his will, his character, his attributes, his disposition, or his purpose, or, to quote once more a definition in the *Oxford English Dictionary*, of the 'disclosure or communication of knowledge to man by a divine or supernatural agency'. I am well aware that many theologians maintain that this ordinary sense of the word is something entirely different from the biblical meaning of revelation. A characteristic example of this view is A. Nygren's distinction between 'two different ways of viewing revelation: (1) the biblical, realistic, active concept, and (2) the intellectualistic concept, which came as a heritage from Greek thought and has held sway for the most part ever since the Enlightenment'.[1] The latter view is further described in the following terms: 'Man has a knowledge now that he formerly lacked. Such is the intellectualistic concept of

---

[1] *The Significance of the Bible for the Church* (Facet Books. Biblical Series 1), Philadelphia 1963, p. 1. The first section of this book is an English version of Nygren's article 'Uppenbarelsen och Skriften' in R. Bring *et al.*, *En bok om bibeln*, 2. uppl., Lund 1948, pp. 85 ff.

revelation. People sometimes say that existence becomes transparent; something of God shines through, in nature, in human life, in history.'[2] '"Revelation" is thought of as the theoretical communication of formerly hidden knowledge.'[3] The biblical idea of revelation is said to be wholly different: quoting Isa. 52.10 and 53.1, Nygren emphasizes that revelation 'is an active intervention of God. God does not sit still as the passive object of our observation. In revelation he is dealing actively with our existence, laying his hand on it and changing its circumstances'. This would seem to mean that my definition of revelation above is unbiblical and altogether unsuitable in a study which concerns also Old Testament material. But on closer consideration Nygren's sharp distinction, so typical of much modern biblical theology, appears to be far from evident and in fact rather misleading. Revelation as communication of knowledge is contrasted with revelation as dynamic divine activity, but it is difficult to see why these two should be incompatible: the first definition seems to have in view a *result* of revelation: that 'man has a knowledge now that he formerly lacked', whereas the second one concerns primarily the *way* this is brought about: through 'an active intervention of God'. It is perfectly possible to hold that revelation consists in a divine activity and also that it gives knowledge of God, and there is no doubt that the biblical view includes both these aspects and cannot be forced into Nygren's alternative.[4] The acts of God do disclose something about his character. A typical passage like Ps. 9.17, נודע יהוה משפט עשה 'Yhwh has made himself known, he has executed judgment', naturally combines an element of knowledge with the dynamic aspect. This is not to say that the sole purpose of the acts of God should be to impart knowledge—of course this purpose must also be described in terms of deliverance, salvation, judgment, etc. But there seems to be no valid reason why the word revelation should not be used in the ordinary, conventional sense for that aspect of the divine activity which involves a disclosure of knowledge or a form of divine (self-)communication. Nor does this mean that revelation is necessarily a central concept, only that it is sometimes a useful one.[5]

---

[2] Op. cit., pp. 1 f. (=En bok om bibeln, pp. 85 f.).

[3] Op. cit., p. 3 (=En bok om bibeln, p. 87).

[4] Cf. the judicious criticism of Nygren's distinction in R. Josefson, Bibelns auktoritet, Stockholm 1953, pp. 98 ff.

[5] F. G. Downing in Has Christianity a Revelation? sometimes seems to operate with an alternative similar to that of Nygren (on Isa. 51.5: 'It is not an insight into God's character that is being "revealed"; it is an activity of God that is coming out into the open', p. 23), but primarily argues that we are not entitled to speak of 'revelation' at all ('God does not reveal himself', p. 45; and passim). This seems largely to be due to an extremely narrow concept of revelation: I do not see how anything

Where men believe in a divine rule over history it is *a priori* likely that they should also believe in a revelation through history. It is natural to think that a person's actions disclose his character and his qualities, and if one believes that what happens in history is ultimately the god's doing, then it seems reasonable to conclude that the events reveal the nature and the disposition of the god. And indeed the idea of the god's activity in history is in the ancient Near East closely connected with the belief that the events reveal something of his character. It is thought to be possible for men to know how the gods are disposed by observing what happens. Just as an unfriendly action in a man indicates that he is angry or injured, so defeats and disasters are interpreted as evidence of the anger or displeasure of the gods, and similarly success and prosperity are held to reveal their favour and mercy.

A well-known example is the so-called Mesha Stone, the inscription of king Mesha of Moab, discovered about a century ago and now in the Louvre. This Moabite king is known also from 2 Kings 3, where he is said to have rebelled against Jehoram of Israel after the death of Ahab. The content of the inscription seems to indicate that it was written toward the end of the king's reign, and it should probably be dated 'between 840 and 820, perhaps about 830 B.C. in round numbers'.[6]

In the beginning of this inscription Mesha says (ll. 4 ff.):[7]

עמרי מלך ישראל ויענו	Omri (was) king of Israel and he
את מאב ימן רבן כי יאנף	humbled Moab for many days, for
כמש בארצה	Chemosh was angry with his land.

Here the defeats in the battles against Israel are interpreted as a sign of the god's wrath. It is clearly stated that it was an earthly adversary, an

---

but the *visio beatifica* could possibly satisfy Downing's definition (see for instance p. 238)—and then of course the concept of revelation becomes unusable *in via*. Barr, in his valuable discussion of the concept of revelation (*Old and New in Interpretation*, pp. 82 ff.), has avoided Downing's exaggerations; his 'argument is not against the word "revelation", but against the way in which the use of this word has grouped together a number of different things in a way that does not suit them and so distorts them' (p. 86); he is not 'denying revelation' (p. 101) but does 'not think that it is a mandatory concept' (p. 86).

[6] W. F. Albright, 'Palestinian Inscriptions', *ANET²*, p. 320. For a discussion of the chronology of the events related in the inscription see A. H. van Zyl, *The Moabites* (Pretoria Oriental Series 3), Leiden 1960, pp. 139 ff.

[7] The edition quoted here is that of W. Röllig in H. Donner–W. Röllig, *Kanaanäische und aramäische Inschriften*, I–III, Wiesbaden 1962–64, no. 181; (text: I, p. 33; German translation and commentary: II, pp. 168 ff.). English renderings of the inscription are found e.g. in *ANET²*, pp. 320 f. (translator: Albright), in *DOTT*, pp. 196 f. (translator: E. Ullendorff), and in van Zyl, op. cit., pp. 189 ff.

Israelite king, that oppressed Moab, but at the same time the god is obviously regarded as the true subject of the action, as Omri's tyranny is treated as evidence of Chemosh's anger. The assumption implied here, that Chemosh acts in history, is clearly expressed in another passage further on in the inscription (ll. 18 ff.):

ומלך ישראל בנה את יהץ	And the king of Israel had built
וישב בה בהלתחמה בי	Jahaz and dwelt in it while
ויגרשה כמש מפני	fighting against me. But Chemosh drove him out before me.

The Mesha Stone indeed 'displays Chemosh "acting in history" in a manner remarkably similar to that of the God of Israel'.[8] Or, to quote another comment on this text: 'The inscription reads, in fact, like a chapter from the O.T. with its alternation of punishment and salvation.'[9] The god acting in history reveals his anger and his mercy.

The affinity of the Moabite Stone to Hebrew accounts of Yhwh's dealings with his people in history is thus striking, but, as we have seen, nothing unique or exceptional. In several of the texts discussed above, describing divine activities in historical events, it is evident that these events were naturally thought to disclose something of the god's nature or attitude. The Sumerian author of 'The Curse of Akkad'[10] was not content to describe the events only, to narrate how Akkad and all Sumer were attacked and ravaged by the Gutians, the barbaric hordes from the mountains in the east; he also asks why this had to happen, he seeks an explanation of the cause behind the disaster.[11] And the answer he found was that Naramsin, the ruler of Akkad, had offended against the commandment of Enlil and had sacked and demolished Ekur, Enlil's shrine in Nippur. Therefore Enlil brought down the Gutians to avenge his temple. Just as the Deuteronomist interprets the fall of Samaria and Jerusalem as Yhwh's punishment for violations of his law, so in the Sumerian text the fall of Akkad is interpreted as a divine judgment upon disobedience and transgression. It is not only that the events are

[8] Barr, *Old and New in Interpretation*, p. 72. Otherwise Barr does not discuss the comparative material; his concern is not so much to question the view that the idea of revelation in history is *distinctive* of the Old Testament as to challenge the notion that it is absolutely central and *typical* of the Bible.

[9] Ullendorff, 'The Moabite Stone', *DOTT*, p. 196. To characterize Chemosh as a 'god of warfare' (van Zyl, op. cit., p. 197) because in the Mesha Stone he is mainly described as active in events of war is hardly justified: the emphasis on the martial trait is due to the contents of the inscription rather than to the god's nature. Cf. above, ch. 1 (especially n. 2).

[10] Above, pp. 24 ff.

[11] Cf. Kramer, *From the Tablets of Sumer*, p. 268.

regarded as divine actions: they are also interpreted as punishment, they are thought to reveal the god's wrath against the king.

In the Era Epic[12] the invasion of hostile hordes is likewise interpreted as a manifestation of divine anger. Like the author of 'The Curse of Akkad', Kabti-ilāni-Marduk seeks to explain why disaster had come, why Babylonia had been reduced to ruins, and like him he finds the answer in the belief that the ravages revealed a god's wrath. In the epic he applies this explanation not only to the fall of Babylon but also, as was pointed out above, to the destruction of Uruk, which is in the fourth tablet regarded as a manifestation of Ishtar's anger.

A passage from Esarhaddon's accounts of the rebuilding of Babylon was quoted above[13] as evidence of the idea of the god's planning and his purposeful activity in history. But it is also evidence of the interpretation of historical events as a revelation of divine wrath or compassion. These inscriptions were probably part of Esarhaddon's endeavours to placate the Babylonian part of his empire,[14] which had suffered grievously under his father, Sennacherib. Naturally he could not simply state that he intended to remedy and restore what his father had destroyed. So the devastation is represented as a divine punishment, the duration of which was shortened through the mercy of Marduk. Defeats and adversities reveal a divine displeasure. Even if Esarhaddon had in the main political intentions with these inscriptions and if, consequently, they do not necessarily express his own personal convictions, they do at any rate presuppose the existence of this belief: politicians may not always be too particular about truth, but they usually see to it that what they say is marketable. And so Esarhaddon must have been able to count on a current belief in historical events as manifestations of divine disfavour or benevolence.

Many years ago Güterbock published a text which is of great interest in this connexion, the so-called Weidner Chronicle,[15] which has been called 'the first Mesopotamian textbook on the idea of history'[16] and 'a milestone in the origins of historiography'.[17] The text is in places ex-

---

[12] Above, pp. 31 ff.

[13] Pp. 91 f.

[14] Cf. Luckenbill, *Ancient Records of Assyria and Babylonia* II, p. 242.

[15] In 'Die historische Tradition und ihre literarische Gestaltung bei Babyloniern und Hethitern bis 1200', ZA 42 (N.F. 8), 1934, pp. 47 ff.

[16] Speiser, 'Ancient Mesopotamia', *The Idea of History in the Ancient Near East*, ed. Dentan, p. 59.

[17] B. C. Brundage, 'The Birth of Clio: A Résumé and Interpretation of Ancient Near Eastern Historiography', *Teachers of History. Essays in Honor of L. B. Packard*, Ithaca, New York 1954, p. 208.

tremely difficult, and much of its contents are still obscure; the beginning is almost entirely illegible. But so much is clear, that this chronicle tells about a series of rulers who do wrong and so lose their thrones. Kingship is a gift of divine favour which may be reclaimed if the god is offended. One of these kings is the famous first ruler of the Dynasty of Akkad, Sargon. He is said to have found favour in the eyes of Marduk and is given kingship over the four quarters of the world. But he commits sin and is dethroned.[18] A similar fate befalls Naramsin: Marduk punishes his transgression by levying hostile armies against him, and they conquer his kingdom. But they in turn incur the divine wrath, and the kingship again passes to a new dynasty. The norm according to which these rulers are judged is their relations to Babylon and above all to the cult of Marduk in the central sanctuary, Esagila. He who sins against this cult and in particular neglects a certain rite is exposed to Marduk's wrath and dethroned. The judgment is entirely anachronistic, as the kings whose destinies are explained in this way by the chronicle reigned long before Babylon and Esagila had yet been built. The interesting thing is not however the lack of historical accuracy in the chronicle but its theology of history: historical events—the falls of kings and dynasties—are interpreted as divine punishment of disobedient princes. History is a revelation of divine judgment. The parallel with Hebrew historians and their view of history as God's judgment on apostate kings is patent.[19] One could perhaps add that they have even the anachronistic trait in common as well as the emphasis on cultic offences: the Weidner Chronicle accuses the kings of sins against a cult which was not yet instituted; the Books of Kings charge rulers in Israel and Judah with violations of the law of the single sanctuary, which came into force long after their time.

The so-called Tukulti-Ninurta Epic may also be mentioned as another clear expression of the belief in historical events as a revelation of divine judgment. It is interesting not least because it is one of the rare examples of native Assyrian literature; most texts are otherwise imitations of Babylonian models.[20] This composition is the only important Assyrian epic known to us, and it gives us an account of how

---

[18] This episode is found in almost identical form also in the so-called Sargon Chronicle (the text published by King, *Chronicles Concerning Early Babylonian Kings* II, London 1907, pp. 113 ff.; a recent English rendering by Oppenheim in *ANET²*, pp. 266 f.). The passage seems to be original in the Weidner Chronicle, from which the Sargon Chronicle has borrowed it: cf. Güterbock, op. cit., pp. 16 f.

[19] Cf. J. J. Finkelstein, 'Mesopotamian Historiography', *PAPhS* 107, 1963, p. 467, n. 24.

[20] Cf. Lambert, 'Three Unpublished Fragments of the Tukulti-Ninurta Epic', *AfO* 18, 1957—58, p. 38.

Tukulti-Ninurta I (1244—1208 B.C.) defeated Kashtiliash IV (1242—1235 B.C.), the Cassite king of Babylonia, and brought this country under Assyrian supremacy for the first time. As in other Mesopotamian texts, the gods are everywhere seen as the true agents in history, and the events are thought to reveal the attitude of the gods—whether favourable or unfavourable—towards the fighting princes. At the beginning the author represents the Babylonian deities as angry with Kashtiliash: because he has broken his oaths they forsake their cities. In a first battle Tukulti-Ninurta is victorious and conquers Babylonia, but Kashtiliash flees and manages to get to a place of safety. Messages are exchanged and the struggle continues. In a great final battle the Assyrian king is assisted by all the gods and afterwards devotes the spoils to the temples of Assyria.[21]

A characteristic episode is the one where Tukulti-Ninurta appeals to Shamash to pronounce the verdict by giving victory to the innocent party:[22]

ša iš-tu maḫ-ra dajjān ab-be-e-ni	Of old thou art the judge of our
la-a muš-pe-lu-ú qu-ra-du at-ta ù	fathers, who changes nothing, a
ša i-na-a[n-n]a a-me-ir ki-na-ti-ni	hero; and still (lit., now) thou
mul-te-še(!)-ru(!) ilu at-ta-ma	art the god who sees our integrity,
	who guides rightly . . .

. . . . .	. . . . .
. . . di-na-an-ni	. . . vindicate me!

. . . . .	. . . . .
[ina an-ni]-ka rabî ana na-ṣir	[By] your great [assent] give
ma-mi-ti li-it kiš-šá-ti šu-ru-	victory over the whole world to
uk[-šu] [la na-ṣir] ši-pa-ri-ka	the one who keeps the oath!
ina a-bi-ik-ti šá tuqunti nišê[meš]	In a defeat in battle des[troy]
[-šu] ḫu[l]-l[i-iq]	the men of him who does not keep
	your decision!

Here the decision of the god is expected to be disclosed in historical events: the outcome of the impending battle will reveal the divine pleasure toward the pious Assyrian king and displeasure with the truce-breaking Cassite ruler.

Oath-breaking is the cause of the divine wrath also in a passage from Ashurbanipal's account of his ninth campaign, against Arabian

---

[21] This brief summary follows the reconstruction suggested by Lambert, op. cit., pp. 40 ff., which is different from the order of columns given in the edition of Ebeling, *Bruchstücke eines politischen Propagandagedichtes aus einer assyrischen Kanzlei* (MAOG 12: 2), Leipzig 1938.

[22] Ebeling, op. cit., p. 19 (col. V (Lambert: II), ll. 17 ff.).

tribes. King Uate cast off the Assyrian yoke and held back his tribute, thereby violating his oath. Ashurbanipal marched against him to suppress the rebellion. In accordance with the current ideology the Assyrian victories are represented as the result of divine activities in history (Rassam Cylinder, col. IX, ll. 53 ff.):[23]

^Iú-a-a-te-' a-di ^{lú}ummânâte-šú ša a-di-ia la iṣ-ṣu-ru šá la-pa-an ^{giš}kakki ^daššur béli-ia ip-par-ši-du-ma in-nab-tu-ni ma-ḫar-šú-nu ú-šam-qit-su-nu-ti ^dèr-ra qar-du su-un-qu ina bi-ri-šú-nu iš-šá-kin-ma a-na bu-ri-šú-nu e-ku-lu šêr mârê^{meš}-šú-nu ina ar-ra-a-ti ma-la ina a-de-e-šú-nu šaṭ-ra ina pit-ti i-ši-mu-šú-nu-ti ^daššur ^dsin ^dšamaš ^dadad ^dbêl ^dnabû ^dištar ša ninua^{ki} ^dšar-rat kid-mu-ri ^dištar ša arba-ilu^{ki} ^dninurta ^dnergal ^dnusku ... niše^{meš kur}a-ri-bi ištên^{en} a-na ištên^{en} iš-ta-na-'-a-lu₄ a-ḫa-meš um-ma ina muḫḫi mi-né-e ki-i ip-še-e-tú an-ni-tú limuttu^{tú} im-ḫu-ru ^{kur}a-ru-bu um-ma áš-šu a-de-e rabûti^{meš} ša ^daššur la ni-iṣ-ṣu-ru ni-iḫ-ṭu-ú ina ṭâbti ^{Id}aššur-bân-aplu šarri na-ram lìb-bi ^den-líl

Era, the warrior, struck down Uate together with his troops, who had not kept the oaths to me, who had fled before the weapons of Ashur, my lord, and had run away before them. Famine broke out among them, and against their hunger they ate the flesh of their children. Ashur, Sin, Shamash, Adad, Bel, Nabu, Ishtar of Nineveh, the Queen of Kidmuri, Ishtar of Arbela, Ninurta, Nergal (and) Nusku instantly visited upon them all the curses written in their sworn treaties (lit., oaths). ... The people of Arabia asked one another: 'Why is it that such calamities have befallen Arabia?' (and answered themselves) thus: 'Because we did not keep the great oaths to Ashur, (because) we have sinned against the kindness of Ashurbanipal, the king, beloved of Enlil's heart.'

The afflictions are thus thought to disclose the divine reaction against violations of a sworn covenant between Assyria and Arabia. Not only the idea of historical calamities as a revelation of a heavenly wrath against a breach of vassal treaties but also the very wording is remarkably reminiscent of some passages in the Old Testament,[24] for instance

---

[23] Streck, *Assurbanipal* II, pp. 76 ff. English translations of this passage are found in Luckenbill, *Ancient Records of Assyria and Babylonia* II, pp. 318 f., and in *ANET²*, pp. 299 f. (translator: Oppenheim).—A shorter parallel version of this passage is found in Ashurbanipal's famous *Gottesbrief*, addressed to Ashur: Streck, op. cit., II, pp. 376 ff.; English translation in Luckenbill, op. cit., II, pp. 367 f.

[24] According to Frankena ('The Vassal-Treaties of Esarhaddon and the Dating of Deuteronomy', כה *1940—1965* (OTS 14), Leiden 1965, p. 153) the similarity shows

Jer. 22.8 f.[25] (cf. also 5.19 and Deut. 29.23 ff.; 1 Kings 9.8 f.; 2 Chr. 7.21 f.):

וְעָבְרוּ גּוֹיִם רַבִּים עַל הָעִיר
הַזֹּאת וְאָמְרוּ אִישׁ אֶל־רֵעֵהוּ
עַל־מֶה עָשָׂה יְהוָה כָּכָה לָעִיר
הַגְּדוֹלָה הַזֹּאת: וְאָמְרוּ עַל
אֲשֶׁר עָזְבוּ אֶת־בְּרִית יְהוָה
אֱלֹהֵיהֶם וַיִּשְׁתַּחֲווּ לֵאלֹהִים
אֲחֵרִים וַיַּעַבְדוּם:

And many people[26] will pass by this city and they will say to one another: 'Why has Yhwh done thus to this great city?' And they will answer: 'Because they have forsaken the covenant of Yhwh their God, and worshipped other gods, and served them.'

We are used to taking such a passage as a distinctive expression of that view of history as judgment which is commonly called 'prophetic': 'when the modern philosopher of history speaks of "the prophetic interpretation of history" it is the doctrine of moral retribution that he has principally in mind.'[27] But this doctrine is in fact a stock interpretation of defeat and disaster in the ancient Near East, as is documented by the Weidner Chronicle, the Tukulti-Ninurta Epic and other Mesopotamian texts adduced above. It may confidently be maintained that 'as a doctrine it is not questioned in any known cuneiform text'.[28]

The same belief is well attested also in the Hittite material. Among the important texts in this connexion are the so-called Plague Prayers of king Mursilis II (1339—1306 B.C.), quoted above as evidence of the idea of a divine rule in history.[29] The occasion for these prayers was a severe plague which had ravaged the country for many years; in addition, rebellious neighbours seized the opportunity to attack the weakened Hittite kingdom. As a matter of course the pestilence is held to be a manifestation of the anger of the gods, especially the Storm-god. But Mursilis has been uncertain about the cause of the divine displeasure. This is made the subject of an oracle. It is established that one of the reasons for the punishment is a fault which was committed

---

that the biblical authors knew the Assyrian text, but this is perhaps not a necessary inference: similar ideas may find similar expression without direct borrowing.

[25] This passage is regarded as a later addition by most commentators. That it predicts the destruction of Jerusalem is not, of course, sufficient reason to ascribe it to a post-exilic editor (cf. Mi. 3.12!), but there are other arguments which make it probable that vv. 8–9 are in fact an insertion: see e.g. Volz, *Der Prophet Jeremia*, ad loc.; Rudolph, *Jeremia*, ad loc.

[26] For this translation (rather than 'many nations') see Volz, loc. cit., and Rudolph, loc. cit.

[27] C. R. North, *The Old Testament Interpretation of History*, London 1946, p. 67.

[28] Lambert, *Babylonian Wisdom Literature*, p. 15.

[29] Above, p. 40.

not by Mursilis but by his father Suppiluliumas. Mursilis then confesses this guilt:

> See now! I have admitted my guilt before the Storm-god (and said): 'It is so. We have done it.' I know for certain that the offence was not committed in my days, that it was committed in the days of my father. . . . But, since the Hattian Storm-god is angry for that reason and people are dying in the Hatti land, I am (nevertheless) making the offerings to the Hattian Storm-god, my lord, on that account. Because I humble myself and cry for mercy, hearken to me, Hattian Storm-god, my lord! Let the plague stop in the Hatti land! . . . Hattian Storm-god, my lord, (and) ye gods, my lords! It is only too true that man is sinful. My father sinned and transgressed against the word of the Hattian Storm-god, my lord. But I have not sinned in any respect. It is only too true, however, that the father's sin falls upon the son. So, my father's sin has fallen upon me. Now, I have confessed before the Hattian Storm-god, my lord, and before the gods, my lords (admitting): 'It is true, we have done it.' And because I have confessed my father's sin, let the soul of the Hattian Storm-god, my lord, and (those) of the gods, my lords, be again pacified![30]

Obviously the plague is thought to reveal the Storm-god's wrath upon the sins of the father. C. J. Gadd has drawn a parallel between this Hittite view of the visitation as a punishment for the transgressions of a previous generation and a passage in 2 Sam. 21, where a famine in David's time is said to have befallen the country because of a crime committed by Saul (v. 1):[31]

ויהי רעב בימי דוד שלש	And there was a famine in the
שנים שנה אחרי שנה	days of David for three years,
ויבקש דוד את־פני יהוה	year after year; and David sought
ויאמר יהוה אל־שאול ואל־	Yhwh's face. And Yhwh said:
בית הדמים על אשר־המית	'Upon Saul and upon his house
את־הגבענים:	(rests) blood,[32] because he slew the Gibeonites.'

---

[30] *ANET²*, p. 395 (translator: Goetze). The Hittite text of this passage is found in Goetze's edition in *Kleinasiatische Forschungen* 1, 1930, pp. 212 ff.

[31] *Ideas of Divine Rule in the Ancient East*, p. 38, n. 2. The same parallel is discussed by A. Malamat, 'Doctrines of Causality in Hittite and Biblical Historiography: a Parallel', *VT* 5, 1955, pp. 1 ff. (apparently independently of Gadd, whom he does not mention). Malamat does not seem to be fully aware that this parallel is ultimately a matter not only of doctrines of causality but of common beliefs in historical events as a revelation of divine judgment.

[32] Read בֵּיתֹה דמים (old orthography for ביתו, as in Moabitic) for MT's בית

The agreements between the Hittite and the Hebrew text are certainly striking: a national disaster, self-evidently interpreted as divine punishment; the king's consultation of the oracle;[33] the answer that a previous generation is guilty. The idea of national misfortune as divine punishment for a collective guilt which transcends the individual generations is an important element of the Deuteronomic view of history, but obviously it is not a distinctive feature.[34]

The view that the events of history reveal the gods' judgment of men, especially of kings, emerges already in the older Hittite documents. The Proclamation of Telipinus[35] contains some clear examples, for instance the following passage (1.63–2.1):[36]

> And when Hantilis had become old and was about to become a god, Zidantas killed Pisenis, the son of Hantilis, along with his (i.e. Pisenis'?) sons, and he killed his foremost subjects. And Zidantas became king. And then the gods avenged the blood of Pisenis. And the gods made Ammunas, his (i.e. Zidantas') son, his enemy; and he killed Zidantas, his father. And Ammunas became king. And then the gods avenged the blood of his father Zidantas; they did not prosper (?) him (or), in his hands, the grain (fields), the orchards (?), the vineyards, the cattle, (and) the sheep. And the (following) countries became hostile to him, . . .

The gods avenge the blood of murdered kings; the course of events is not in the hands of unscrupulous princes desirous of power but ultimately governed by the gods, whose punishing justice is in the end revealed in history.

It should perhaps be emphasized here that the idea of historical events as a revelation of divine punishment for sin presupposes not only that the gods act in history but also that they do so according to certain moral principles. If a defeat or the fall of a dynasty is regarded not only as the manifestation of divine anger but as anger at some

---

הדמים: see S. R. Driver, *Notes on the Hebrew Text and the Topography of the Books of Samuel . . .*, 2nd ed., Oxford 1913, ad loc. Cf. also BH³.

[33] This is of course the meaning of the Hebrew text as well: cf. already the Vulgate: *et consuluit David oraculum Domini.*

[34] Cf. Brundage's comment: 'In the moving and pathetic Plague Prayer of Mursilis the sins of the father are visited upon the son in true Biblical fashion' (op. cit., p. 219).

[35] Cf. above, p. 38.

[36] Sturtevant–Bechtel, *A Hittite Chrestomathy*, pp. 185 ff. Cf. on this text also Güterbock, 'Die historische Tradition und ihre literarische Gestaltung bei Babyloniern und Hethitern bis 1200', ZA 44 (N.F. 10), 1938, p. 138.

transgression or negligence, then this implies also the view that the universe is in some way governed according to the laws of justice; it rules out the conception that the gods' actions are nothing but arbitrariness and whimsicality. And indeed this belief in a moral order seems to have been one of the important elements of Mesopotamian religion: 'Israel came into being in a millennium when the concept of a moral universe had been achieved and when men could enter into a covenant of social justice with God as acting in History under which to live collectively and individually in moral responsibility.'[37] In Mesopotamia, as in Israel, the idea of historical events as a revelation of divine wrath or mercy for sins or godliness presupposes both that the deity acts in history and that the universe is ruled with justice.

In his Old Testament Theology von Rad[38] has maintained that in the early time of the monarchy there occurred a radical transformation of the Israelite understanding of Yhwh's activity in history. According to the older traditions Yhwh is revealed above all in extraordinary events, in miracles and in dramatic catastrophes. Yhwh's manifestations in history are seen as isolated, individual acts, clearly distinguished from the normal course of everyday events. Gradually however the Israelites learnt to see Yhwh at work also in less sensational happenings, to believe in a divine guidance of the evolution of events, exercised not through miraculous interventions but in an almost imperceptible, hidden way. This new understanding of the divine rule of history is clearly seen for instance in the Yahwist's work or in the Court History in 2 Sam. Perhaps von Rad is slightly overstating the case for a basically new insight in the Solomonic age: after all we do not know much about whether this view was held before the Yahwist's time or not. It may well have been implicit in the traditions he used and reshaped; and if the old historical traditions preserved primarily the memories of signal events, this is in fact what such oral traditions tend to do: these episodes may have been remembered just because they were exceptional, not because they were the *only* ones in which Yhwh was seen at work, and so we are not necessarily justified in concluding that Yhwh was not then thought to be active in the course of less spectacular events as well. Nevertheless von Rad's distinction between these two ways of divine revelation in history is interesting and important, and may well be applied to the extra-biblical material too. When Israel's neighbours stated their belief in the gods' actions in history which revealed their

---

[37] T. Jacobsen, 'Ancient Mesopotamian Religion: the Central Concerns', *PAPhS* 107, 1963, p. 484.
[38] *Theologie des AT* I, pp. 58 ff.

power, wrath and mercy, did they then point to exceptional occurrences only, which were necessarily the result of a divine intervention, or to the course of ordinary events as well, where nothing miraculous broke the chain of cause and effect?

It is clear already from the passages which have been quoted in the previous chapters that the gods were believed to be at work not only in catastrophic events but also in quite normal occurrences. What von Rad calls 'Jahwes Allkausalität'[39] is hardly a distinctive Israelite conception; it seems possible to speak of a general Near Eastern belief in a kind of divine omnipotence,[40] and this includes the view that all that happens —not only the miraculous—is ultimately caused and controlled by heavenly powers. As this seems to be a time-honoured and widespread conception in the ancient Near East, it would be surprising if it were this conception as such that was a novelty in Israel in the days of David and Solomon: what is new is rather the brilliant way of expressing this belief in historical works of a first-rate literary quality, not the basic insight itself.

One of the most striking non-biblical representations of the view that the ordinary course of events, without any visible divine interventions, reveals the deity's guidance and power is the well-known Apology or Autobiography of the Hittite king Hattusilis III (1275—1250 B.C.),[41] in which he gives an account of his rise to power. The story begins with the king's childhood; he was the last of the four children of king Mursilis II, whose Plague Prayers have been discussed above. He then describes in considerable detail his campaigns and other events during the reign of his brother king Muwatallis (1306—1282 B.C.), under whom he served as a general and governor of the north-eastern provinces. Muwatallis was succeeded by his son Urhi-Teshub, and that was the beginning of the course of events which is the principal subject of the apology: the controversies between the young king and his uncle. Hattusilis claims to have been patient and endured insults and injustices for a long time out of respect for his deceased brother, but finally he revolted, dethroned Urhi-Teshub, and banished him to a distant province. Hattusilis then reigned for a quarter of a century. Now the interesting thing is that the whole series of events which eventually

---

[39] Op. cit., p. 61, with reference to B. Balscheit, *Alter und Aufkommen des Monotheismus in der israelitischen Religion* (BZAW 69), Berlin 1938, pp. 40, 81, 91 f., 125.
[40] Cf. above, p. 23.
[41] Text and German translation in Goetze, *Hattušiliš. Der Bericht über seine Thronbesteigung nebst den Paralleltexten* (MVAG 29: 3), Leipzig 1925; text and English translation in Sturtevant–Bechtel, op. cit., pp. 42 ff. Cf. also Gurney, *The Hittites*, pp. 175 ff.

made Hattusilis king of the Hittites is described as a *Führungsge-schichte*; the elaborate account of the usurper's road to power is introduced with the words 'I tell Ishtar's divine power; let mankind hear it'.[42] Gese's words about the Apology of Hattusilis might as well have been taken from von Rad's characterization of the new understanding of Yhwh's action in history in the early period of the monarchy: 'Es wird nicht von grossartigen Wundern und Mirakeln berichtet, sondern einfach Geschehenes beschrieben. Nur wird diese Geschichte als Führung durch die Gottheit interpretiert.'[43] From the very beginning, when, as a child, he was dedicated to Ishtar, his career had been furthered by the goddess, who always made him prevail against his adversaries, however unpropitious the prospects. History—not only supernatural events and remarkable occurrences but ordinary political and military history, where kings and generals seem to be the only agents—is ultimately guided by the goddess and can be understood as a revelation of her divine power.

Though the Apology of Hattusilis expresses this view in a particularly striking way, it is far from unique in Hittite literature: for instance the Annals of Mursilis II, the father of Hattusilis, often describe a successful military campaign or the misfortunes of vassals who have broken their oaths—all perfectly regular occurrences—as a manifestation of the divine power.[44]

It is often maintained that the Hebrews alone among the peoples of

---

[42] 1: 5 f.; Sturtevant–Bechtel, op. cit., p. 65. Cf. Goetze's translation: 'Der Ištar Walten will ich berichten, und jedermann soll davon hören' (op. cit., p. 7). The Hittite name of the goddess is not known; the cuneiform text has the sign used for Ishtar. The expression which has been rendered 'divine power' and 'Walten' is the Hittite *parā ḫandandātar*, a noun which 'is everywhere an attribute to deities, and denotes the superhuman power in virtue of which the are able to perform wondrous deeds' (Gurney, 'Hittite Prayers of Mursili II', *AAA* 27, 1940, p. 76); cf. Goetze's definition: 'schicksalsbestimmende Kraft der Götter, göttliches Walten' (op. cit., p. 52, with a detailed discussion of the etymology and meaning of the word).

[43] 'Geschichtliches Denken im Alten Orient und im Alten Testament', *ZThK* 55, 1958, p. 140. Cf. Goetze: 'Als Manifestationen der Götter werden Phänomene interpretiert, die den Menschen durch überirdische Gewalt oder durch übernatürlich anmutendes Auftreten beeindrucken: eine feurige Erscheinung am Himmel, der Einsturz einer Mauer in einer belagerten Stadt. Man kann sie nur als eine Äusserung der übermenschlichen Kraft der Götter, ihrer *para handandatar*, verstehen. Einmal aufmerksam geworden auf Zeichen und Portenta dieser Art, war es nur ein kleiner Schritt, nun in allen möglichen Geschehnissen, auch in weniger auffälligen und schliesslich in ganz harmlosen, die Stimme der Götter zu vernehmen.' (*Kleinasien*, Handbuch der Altertumswissenschaft, III. I. 3. 3. 1), 2. Aufl., München 1957, p. 148.)

[44] See Goetze, *Die Annalen des Muršiliš*, e.g. Obv. II.76 f. (p. 123) or Rev. IV.11 ff. (p. 193); both passages speak of *parā hand(and)ātar*.

the ancient Near East were capable of interpreting a defeat and the destruction of city and temple by enemies not as a token of the god's weakness but as a revelation of his power and punishing wrath. A characteristic example of this common opinion is found in an article on the Israelite conception of God by E. Würthwein: 'Den genuin israelitischen Glauben, dass Jahwe sich in der Geschichte seines Volkes offenbart, führen sie [i.e. the prophets] mit innerer Logik weiter zur Verkündigung Jahwes als des Herrn der Weltgeschichte. ... Sie wagen die für antikes Denken paradoxe Aussage, dass der Niedergang Israels nicht die Schwäche, sondern die Grösse seines Gottes, Jahwes Weltüberlegenheit und Heiligkeit bezeugt, und führen damit den Gottesglauben zu echtem Universalismus.'[45] This is, I think, somewhat misleading: far from being a paradox the prophetic interpretation of the collapse of Israel seems to be wholly in line with the common Near Eastern view of such events. A passage from the basalt stele of Nabonidus is an illustrative example. In the historical introduction to his account of his rise to power, Nabonidus also describes how Sennacherib ravaged Babylon and destroyed its sanctuaries. But this is not at all taken as evidence of Marduk's weakness: on the contrary the catastrophe revealed his powerful wrath against the inhabitants of his own city (col. I, ll. 18 ff.):[46]

ki-ma uz-zi ili-ma i-te-pu-uš mâta ul ip-šú-ur [ki]-mil-ta-šu rubû ᵈmarduk 21 šanâti qé-reb aššur^ki ir-ta-me šu-bat-su [i]m-lu-ú ûmê^meš ik-šu-da a-dan-nu i-nú-úḫ-ma uz-za-šu šá šar ilâni bêl bêlê é-sag-ila u bâb-ili^ki iḫ-su-us šu-bat be-lu-ti-šú	According to the wrath of the god he (i.e. Sennacherib) did (this) against the land. The prince Marduk did not appease his anger. For 21 years he settled down in Ashur. (But) the days became full, the time arrived (and) the wrath of the king of the gods, the lord of lords, calmed down; he remembered Esagila and Babylon, the seat of his lordship.

Sennacherib was but an instrument in the hand of the wrathful god of the destroyed city, and even his carrying away of Marduk's statue is interpreted as the god's voluntary exile. We are not far here from the Old Testament understanding of the fall of Jerusalem as a testimony not of Yhwh's impotence but of his power to use even the mighty ruler

---

[45] 'Gott. II. In Israel', RGG³ II, col. 1710.
[46] Langdon–Zehnpfund, *Die neubabylonischen Königsinschriften*, p. 270 f. (transliteration and German translation). For an English rendering see Oppenheim in *ANET²*, p. 309.

of a foreign empire to execute his judgment upon an apostate people. The text is admittedly late, but the conception itself is ancient and in fact goes back to the Sumerians. We have met this understanding of the destruction of a city in the Sumerian 'Curse of Akkad',[47] in the Era Epic[48] and in the inscriptions of Esarhaddon,[49] to mention only a few examples from widely different periods of Mesopotamian history. Thus desolation is not interpreted as a sign of divine wrath in general or of the power of the invaders' gods: it is understood as the wrath of the stricken nation's own deity, it is held to reveal the god's judgment upon his own people and his own abode.[50]

In many works on the Old Testament the emphasis is so strongly on the *medium* of revelation, history, that the question of *what* is revealed seems at times to be somewhat neglected. The question of the content of a revelation which is given in the form of historical events is however not unimportant. It is evident from the non-biblical texts discussed above that what is held to be revealed through the manifold events of history is not more than a few basic things: the god's superhuman power, his anger or his favourable disposition. That is all; the content of this revelation is in fact rather limited. On closer consideration, however, the same seems to be true also of the Old Testament. L. Köhler, in his Old Testament Theology, has made an observation which is important for the understanding of the Israelite view of revelation but which has been largely disregarded by the advocates of the current opinion that God makes himself known chiefly through his acts in history. Köhler writes:[51] 'Dass Gott sich durch seine Werke, seien es die der Natur, seien es die der Geschichte, offenbart, ist ein durch ungemein viele Beispiele belegtes Theologumenon. Gering ist die Fülle der Offenbarungsinhalte. Es ist nicht viel mehr als der Satz, dass Jahwe Gott ist, der die Welt nach seinem Willen lenkt, Israel seine Liebe zuwendet Dtn 11.2–7 und es straft, wenn es sein muss Hes 39.23. Dagegen ist die Fülle der Werke, durch die Gott sich offenbart, gross und bunt. Auch die Zahl der Empfänger ist gross ...' The agree-

---

[47] Esp. ll. 60 ff.; above p. 25.
[48] E.g. IV.60 ff.; above p. 33.
[49] Above p. 102.
[50] Cf. Oppenheim's comment on an omen mentioning the destruction of the temple É-giš-nu$_x$-gal: 'Diese Zerstörung des Sintempels in Ur fand sicherlich bei der Eroberung durch die Elamier statt, die eben das Ende der Stadt und des Reiches herbeiführte. Nach altorientalischer Auffassung konnte ein solches Heiligtum, das Zentrum des mesopotamischen Sinkultus, einzig und allein auf Befehl des Herrn dieses Tempel und zum Zweck der Bestrafung seiner sündigen oder ungehorsamen Verehrer vernichtet werden.' ('Zur keilschriftlichen Omenliteratur', *Or* N.S. 5, 1936, p. 220).
[51] *Theologie des Alten Testaments*, Tübingen 1936, p. 84.

ment on this point between the Old Testament and the documents of the neighbouring peoples is notable: they all speak of a great variety of historical events interpreted as divine acts in history, and these manifold events are all held to reveal the same few things: the power, mercy or wrath of the god. 'Gering ist die Fülle der Offenbarungsinhalte.'

But once this is seen—and there appears to be no possibility of escaping the fact—the contention that revelation in history is a distinctive conception of the Old Testament becomes still more difficult to uphold. If historical events as a *medium* of revelation is a general Near Eastern conception and the limited *content* of a revelation conveyed through this medium is conceived in much the same way both by the Israelites and by their neighbours, then there is very little foundation indeed for the common claim to distinctiveness on this particular point.

It does not follow that we shall have to give up the idea of Israelite religion as in vital respects different from the other religions of the ancient Near East.[52] No one who has read both the Old Testament and some documents from Israel's environment can fail to feel a fundamental difference between the faiths expressed in the texts, and this impression is in a way even strengthened by the numerous and striking similarities. To define this indisputable distinctiveness is an important and difficult task, and no simple slogan will suffice. But this much at any rate is clear, that the Old Testament idea of historical events as divine revelation must be counted among the similarities, not among the distinctive traits: it is part of the common theology of the ancient Near East.[53]

---

[52] Nor does it follow that the exclusive position of Hebrew historiography must be denied. It is an indisputable fact that the Old Testament contains historiographical works to which it is difficult to find real parallels in the ancient Near East, and this fact is not, of course, affected by the results reached above. What is affected is a common attempt to specify the reason why the Israelites excelled their neighbours in this genre. The explanation usually given is that the Hebrews alone conceived of history as the sphere of divine activity; a unique religious idea gave rise to a unique historiography (so for instance Mowinckel, 'Israelite Historiography', *ASTI* 2, 1963, p. 8: 'It is commonly agreed that this history-mindedness is due to the peculiar character of its [i.e. Israel's] religion. Israel had from the beginning experienced its God as one who works through real historical events.'). But if the main argument of the present essay is sound, this explanation would seem to require modification: the Israelite idea of historical events as divine manifestations is not unique and so is hardly sufficient to explain the unique character of Hebrew historical narrative. The reason why the Hebrews produced historiography on a level unknown in their environment must probably be sought elsewhere. But that is a problem which lies beyond the scope of the present investigation.

[53] Cf. the title of an article by M. Smith, 'The Common Theology of the Ancient Near East' (*JBL* 71, 1952, pp. 135 ff.).

Concluding Remarks

It seems unnecessary to summarize here the main results of the present study; they should be clear enough. But on the basis of these results some brief concluding remarks may perhaps be offered; they are intended merely as suggestions about possible implications and further lines of inquiry.

Even if the idea of divine acts in history is found in much the same form both in Israel and in the neighbouring peoples, it may well have occupied a rather different place in the different patterns of beliefs. It is however difficult to reach any positive results on such a point. The Hebrew material may be reasonably sufficient for an analysis of the place of a certain idea within the framework of the Old Testament faith, but this is hardly true about e.g. the Mesopotamian material: the accidental character of the selection of texts and many other difficulties make most attempts to assess the relative importance of different conceptions and beliefs extremely precarious.[1] What we can do is to establish the presence or non-presence of a certain idea in the available material; any further steps are difficult and hazardous.

One thing may however be stated with some confidence: it would seem that the idea of historical events as divine manifestations has marked the Israelite cult in a way that lacks real parallels among Israel's neighbours. The important rôle that the commemoration of Yhwh's deeds in history plays in Hebrew worship is well known and need not be analysed here; one of the most characteristic features is the 'historicising' of originally agrarian feasts.[2] It may be a significant fact that it has not been possible to quote any Ugaritic texts above among the evidence for the general Near Eastern idea of a divine rule and a divine revelation in history, for the simple reason that no passages which

---

[1] For a discussion—'predominantly negative in tone and outlook'—of the possibilities of a structural evaluation of Mesopotamian religion see Oppenheim, *Ancient Mesopotamia*, pp. 171 ff.

[2] See e.g. von Rad, *Theologie des AT* II, pp. 117 f.

express this idea are found in these texts.[3] Now it would certainly be rash and an impermissible inference *e silentio* to conclude that the belief in the gods' activities in historical events was unknown in Ugarit: an idea so well-known and widespread in the ancient Near East is highly unlikely to have been wanting there. The reason is probably rather to be sought in the character of these texts: they are cult texts, and that is why we do not find any evidence of a belief in the divine activity in history. But then it is noteworthy that even if we limit the Old Testament material to cult texts it will still testify to this belief. This may be taken to indicate a significant difference between Ugaritic and Israelite worship. The division between other neighbouring peoples and Israel on this point is perhaps not quite as clear-cut. The evidence cited above for the idea of history as the gods' field of action includes some cultic texts, and the divine deeds in history are commemorated in epithets used in the invocation of Mesopotamian deities: as Yhwh was extolled in the hymns as the deliverer of his people from the power of the Egyptians, so these gods were praised as the destroyers of the hostile mountain countries.[4] Nevertheless it appears evident that the deity's saving acts in history are nowhere afforded so central a position in the cult as in Israel, where they dominate the Passover and other ancient feasts. This, then, is a field where we may be entitled to speak of something distinctive. The distinctiveness is not, however, found in the conception as such but in its relative importance, its capacity for influencing the cult.

At the same time the fact that Yhwh's saving acts in history are commemorated in the cult involves certain problems precisely with regard to their quality as historical events. It may be argued that in so far as the events are incorporated into the cult they tend to lose their character as historical occurrences, their *Einmaligkeit,* and acquire a kind of timelessness. From one point of view there is little difference between Marduk's creation of the world as experienced in the Babylonian cult and Yhwh's victory over Egypt in the Exodus as experienced

---

[3] J. Gray has attempted to show ('Social Aspects of Canaanite religion', *Volume du Congrès, Genève 1965* (SupplVT 15), Leiden 1966, pp. 170 ff.) that 'El's province was social relationships rather than nature' (p. 179), but in any case there seems to be no clear evidence of the idea of historical events as divine actions. One text (Gordon, *UH* 2) is taken as evidence of the belief that a certain calamity is the result of a divine anger (p. 189), but this interpretation is based on a hypothetical reconstruction of a badly mutilated text.

[4] Cf. Falkenstein: 'Die ständige Bedrohung Babyloniens durch die Nachbarländer hat im immer wiederkehrenden Preis der Heldengottheiten, die „das Bergland vernichten", einen sprechenden Ausdruck erhalten.' (Falkenstein–von Soden, *Sumerische und akkadische Hymnen und Gebete,* p. 36).

in the Israelite cult: both events are lifted out of the context of ordinary occurrences, and it is significant that the exodus event is described in terms and categories borrowed from the creation myth. The historical narrative becomes a myth, in the technical meaning of a ritual text, but this inevitably means that its historical character is diluted. Thus the incident which is understood as a divine revelation is, by being re-experienced in the eternal 'now' of the cult, in a way losing its primary character of a historical event. This creates a new difficulty: where, then, are we to place the *locus* of revelation: in the original historical occurrence, or in the cultic experience of it? Perhaps the ancient Israelites would not have understood the question, and in fact the alternatives may not be mutually exclusive.[5] But it is still worth noticing that the very fact that historical events were important enough to be afforded a central position in the Israelite cult also contributes to the dissolution of their historical character.

Another difficulty is implied in the observation that the content of a revelation given through the events of history must in fact be rather restricted, as was pointed out in the previous chapter. Little reflection is needed to perceive that this must be so. The events themselves are naturally mute in many vital respects. They may, as we have seen, reveal the deity's power, his anger or pleasure, but they cannot possibly disclose his reasons and causes, purposes and intentions. This is already clear from many extra-biblical sources. To Mursilis II the plague raging in his country has revealed that the Storm-god must be angry with the Hittites, but the bare events do not tell him the reason for the divine punishment: he must ask for further information on this point through other media of revelation:[6]

---

[5] In an interesting paper R. Gyllenberg maintains 'dass die kultische Offenbarung in einem mit Zukunft und Vergangenheit geladenen Augenblick in der Gegenwart erteilt wird, dadurch aber auch einen selbständigen Wert der Geschichte als Stätte der Offenbarung ausschliesst' ('Kultus und Offenbarung', *Interpretationes ad Vetus Testamentum pertinentes Sigmundo Mowinckel septuagenario missae*, Oslo 1955, p. 78). But Gyllenberg's somewhat one-sided emphasis on the cult seems to me to obscure the vital fact that the very reason why the saving events were re-presented in the *cult* was that they were held to have been revelatory as *historical* events. The cult not only obscures but also presupposes the historical character of the events, and we must do justice to both aspects of this seemingly paradoxical statement—otherwise we shall end up in a Bultmannian error.

[6] *ANET*[2], pp. 394 f. The three media of revelation mentioned here, omen, dream, and prophet, are precisely the same as in 1 Sam. 28.6: וישאל שאול ביהוה ולא ענהו יהוה גם בחלמות גם באורים גם בנביאם : 'And Saul inquired of Yhwh, but Yhwh did not answer him, either by dreams, or by *urim*, or by prophets.'

'... The reason for which people are dying in the Hatti land—
either let it be established by an omen, or let me see it in a dream,
or let a prophet declare it!' But the gods did not hearken to me
and the plague got no better in the Hatti land.

The same is true also on a different level, in the Old Testament. Yhwh's
redemptive acts in history, his saving deeds in Exodus and Conquest
may reveal that he is benevolent towards the Hebrews, but these events
are not enough to reveal his deepest intentions, the basic motive for his
benefaction. Was it because of the faithfulness of the Hebrews, their
piety and righteousness—or is the reason to be found in God's own
secret heart, in his inscrutable love for an insignificant and unworthy
nation? The difference between these two alternatives is immense: it
is the difference between law and gospel, between man's merits and
undeserved divine grace. But no naked events will decide which alternative is right; they are mute—or rather, they are ambiguous. Something must be given in addition to the events: the *word* of revelation,
which may be about history but cannot simply be deduced from history.
That Yhwh chose Israel out of all the nations on the earth and redeemed
it from the house of bondage not because of the people's qualifications
but because of his own love and faithfulness (Deut. 7.6 ff.; cf. 10.14 f.)
cannot be discovered from the course of events, from the deeds themselves, but has to be revealed in a verbal communication, in words. To
state that the 'doctrine of election was an inference from historical
events'[7] is highly inadequate as a description of the Old Testament's
own representation. The election was announced to the patriarchs and
to Moses through Yhwh's own words. And what events could possibly
reveal that Yhwh will give his servant Israel as a light to the nations,
to make his salvation reach to the end of the earth (Isa. 49.6)? This
can be known only if Yhwh himself speaks his word to the prophet.
Such divine words are by no means a rare medium of revelation in the
Old Testament: on the contrary, it is said time and again that Yhwh
speaks, directly or through his messenger, disclosing his will, his demand
and his purpose to man. Lindblom has rightly emphasized that this idea
of Yhwh's speaking is very prominent in the Old Testament:[8] in all
ages, in all literary genres and in the most different connexions we
hear how God has spoken to man; and Lindblom also points out how

---

[7] Wright, *God Who Acts*, p. 51.
[8] 'Die Vorstellung vom Sprechen Jahwes zu den Menschen im Alten Testament',
ZAW 75 (N.F. 34), 1963, pp. 263 ff. See also Barr, 'Revelation Through History in
the Old Testament and in Modern Theology', *Interpretation* 17, 1963, esp. pp. 197;
201 f.

natural this conception is: 'durch das Sprechen kommt ja das Wesen einer Persönlichkeit besser zum Ausdruck als durch andere Lebensäusserungen.'[9]

Many of these divine messages do concern history. But clearly we ought not to call this revelation *in* history:[10] it is rather a revelation *about* history. The distinction is no doubt rather trivial and self-evident, but it does not seem to be altogether superfluous to lay some stress upon it, as revelation in history and revelation about history are in fact constantly confused. It is for instance very common to speak about 'history as the revelation of divine purpose'[11] as if the divine purpose had been revealed through the events themselves. It should however be evident that as a rule this is not the case: the bare facts of history are usually capable of several different interpretations, and the inner meaning of the events, Yhwh's purpose behind the occurrences, is not clear unless it is disclosed in words which Yhwh speaks to his chosen messengers. And this is, of course, how the Old Testament itself represents the matter: Israel's knowledge of God's purposes in history is not obtained through history but through the divine word about history. This is true also of the few cases where it might conceivably have been possible to say that the course of history itself had revealed a divine purpose. In certain sequences of events the final outcome may have served as a sort of key to the whole process, for instance in the Yahwist's work or other cases of history written from the standpoint of the attained goal, but even there this is not the picture presented by the Old Testament narrators themselves: they have not gradually become aware of Yhwh's aims by meditating upon past events but know of divine promises and other verbal communications which have disclosed the final goal in advance.

The revelation in words, then, necessarily plays an important rôle. But even when this is recognized, the relation between event and word is often incorrectly described. The true revelatory character must at all costs be reserved for 'history', for the events, and so it is customary to

---

[9] Op. cit., p. 263.

[10] The phrase 'revelation in history' is ambiguous in a way which may have contributed to its popularity: besides meaning 'revelation through historical events' (as against nature, the word, and other media) it may of course mean 'revelation received at a particular moment in the course of history', but as revelation is, by definition, a communication to *man*, this is simply tautological: every conceivable revelation must be 'in history' in this sense.

[11] The wording is taken from Brandon, *History, Time and Deity*, p. 106 (the title of ch. 5), but similar formulations may be found in many authors: cf. for instance H. H. Guthrie, Jr., *God and History in the Old Testament*, London 1961, p. 35: the 'purpose had slowly been revealed in the events . . .'.

represent the words as a subsequent interpretation of events already occurred. Thus the word is not allowed to be an independent medium of divine revelation, only a derivative one. An illustrative example is afforded in an interesting and suggestive inaugural lecture by D. E. Nineham.[12] He is aware that what has happened in history is capable of different interpretations and that something must be given in addition to the events themselves. This is made clear by means of an illuminative analogy, a story about a man who wanted to find out all he could about a millionaire who was personally unknown to him.[13] Certain things that the rich man has done seem to reveal a good deal about his nature and character. But something more is needed: the 'acts will not be revelatory at all unless we have an authoritative account of their meaning, which must ultimately be derived from the millionaire himself.'[14] In plain language: unless we have not only historical events but also authoritative words about these events very little will be revealed. Now the interesting and characteristic thing in Nineham's lecture is that these words are all the time simply described as an interpretation of past events; the primary thing is always the event, and the word is in all respects secondary. It is most typical that Nineham discusses only two alternative views of revelation: one which puts the emphasis on 'the events themselves as the primary *locus* of revelation' and another which holds 'that the locus of revelation is in fact the events-as-interpreted-by-the-inspired-writers'.[15] That is to say, even the alternative which does reckon with a revelation through words degrades them to something derivative: first comes the revelatory event, then the interpretation of it. Or, with another characteristic formulation: 'the divine self-revelation was and is mediated through historical event and inspired meditation thereon.'[16]

Against this it must be emphasized that not only does God speak to man according to the Old Testament: he also does so *before* his great deeds in history.[17] To represent the verbal aspect of the divine self-revelation as merely a subsequent interpretation of events already occurred is entirely foreign to the Old Testament authors.[18] The most

---

[12] *The Study of Divinity. An Inaugural Lecture* . . ., London 1960.

[13] Op. cit., pp. 9 ff.

[14] Op. cit., p. 16; cf. p. 11.

[15] Op. cit., p. 16.

[16] C. A. Simpson, 'An Inquiry into the Biblical Theology of History', *JTS* N.S. 12, 1961, p. 1.

[17] Cf. Rendtorff, 'Geschichte und Wort im Alten Testament', *EvTh* 22, 1962, pp. 626 ff.; Barr, op. cit., pp. 197; 201 f.

[18] Rendtorff points out 'dass niemals berichtet wird, dass ein Prophet oder ein

central of all Yhwh's redemptive and revelatory acts in history is the Exodus. But even here the revelation in the divine word is vital and indeed primary: 'Far from the incident at the burning bush being an "interpretation" of the divine acts, it is a direct communication from God to Moses of his purposes and intentions. This conversation, instead of being represented as an interpretation of the divine act, is a precondition of it. If God had not told Moses what he did, the Israelites would not have demanded their escape from Egypt, and the deliverance at the Sea of Reeds would not have taken place.'[19]

The same holds good also of the Old Testament prophets. It is true that they often interpret contemporary events or recall Yhwh's acts in Israel's past, but we have so often been told that they are not fore-tellers but forth-tellers that it is easy to forget how much their preaching does in fact concern future events. Fore-telling and forth-telling are not, of course, mutually exclusive: what the prophets do is to a large extent to speak to their contemporaries about what Yhwh is going to do in days to come; present iniquities are scourged with the threat of a future judgment. But obviously in such cases it is not primarily the event that constitutes the divine revelation, because both the event and its meaning, Yhwh's purpose behind what happens, have already been revealed in Yhwh's word, proclaimed by the prophet before the event. 'Das Geschehen ist verwirklichtes Wort, eingelöste Verkündigung.'[20] This does not mean that the occurrence itself becomes less important: naturally the promise or the threat is not fulfilled until what is promised or threatened has really happened, but it does mean that the element of *revelation* is to be found in the oracle proclaiming the event rather than in the event itself, in the word about history rather than in history.

Thus the relation between divine deed and divine word is not only, nor even predominantly, that of a mute event to which an interpretative oracle has simply been added. The interplay of word and event is sometimes rather complicated and subtle; the highly developed narrative technique of Old Testament historiographers, for instance, often allows them to bring out the meaning of an episode or a course of events not by adding a direct interpretation in the form of a divine utterance but indirectly, by inserting the events in a continuity or context where the very perspective adds significance to the individual incident. But even so this perspective is ultimately determined by

---

anderer von Jahwe beauftragter Sprecher nachträglich ein Ereignis als Handeln Jahwes gedeutet habe' (op. cit., p. 631).
[19] Barr, op. cit., p. 197.
[20] Zimmerli, '„Offenbarung" im Alten Testament', *EvTh* 22, 1962, p. 25.

Yhwh's promises[21] or threats[22] from days of old. It remains true that events alone are not capable of expressing those ideas of Hebrew religion which are truly distinctive; the Old Testament view of the divine deed is not possible without the divine word.

This divine word is presented in a variety of forms, both with and without reference to events, as promises or demands, predictions or interpretations of Israel's past history. The form of this revelation is not distinctive: it is a common belief that the deity speaks to man, and prophets claiming to reveal divine messages are known also outside Israel.[23] But the content of this revelation is in several respects unique. It is here that we learn about Yhwh's purposes and intentions, his true nature and the innermost thoughts of his heart, his gifts and his claims, which make him different from all the other gods of the ancient Near East.

So the specific content of the Hebrew faith—that which goes beyond the ideas of divine power, pleasure, or wrath which bare events are capable of revealing and which are a common heritage of ancient Near Eastern religions—is, in the last resort, derived from what the Old Testament represents as a divine revelation through the word. That is why the exaggerated emphasis on historical events as a distinctive and supreme medium of revelation, which is characteristic of much contemporary Old Testament theology, requires modification. Both the extra-biblical material and the Old Testament itself demand it.

---

[21] See for instance above, p. 81.

[22] See for instance above, pp. 82 f.

[23] See e.g. the excellent survey by Nötscher, 'Prophetie im Umkreis des alten Israel', BZ N.F. 10, 1966, pp. 161 ff.

Abbreviations

AAA	*Annals of Archaeology and Anthropology*
AB	The Anchor Bible
AfO	*Archiv für Orientforschung*
AHw	*Akkadisches Handwörterbuch. Unter Benutzung des lexikalischen Nachlasses von Bruno Meissner (1868–1947) bearbeitet von Wolfram von Soden*, Wiesbaden 1959–
ANET²	J. Pritchard (ed.), *Ancient Near Eastern Texts Relating to the Old Testament*, 2nd ed., Princeton 1955
AO	Der alte Orient
AOB	Altorientalische Bibliothek
AOS	American Oriental Series
AS	*Anatolian Studies*
ASTI	*Annual of the Swedish Theological Institute*
ATD	Das Alte Testament Deutsch
AV	The Authorized Version
BASOR	*Bulletin of the American Schools of Oriental Research*
BDB	F. Brown—S. R. Driver—C. A. Briggs, *A Hebrew and English Lexicon of the Old Testament*, Oxford 1907
BH³	R. Kittel (ed.), *Biblia Hebraica*, 3rd ed., Stuttgart 1937
BiOr	*Bibliotheca Orientalis*
BKAT	Biblischer Kommentar Altes Testament
BWANT	Beiträge zur Wissenschaft vom Alten und Neuen Testament
BZ	*Biblische Zeitschrift*
BZAW	Beihefte zur *Zeitschrift für die alttestamentliche Wissenschaft*
CAD	*The Assyrian Dictionary of the University of Chicago*, Chicago 1956–
CBQ	*Catholic Biblical Quarterly*
CuW	*Christentum und Wissenschaft*
DOTT	D. W. Thomas (ed.), *Documents from Old Testament Times*, London ... 1958
DTT	*Dansk Teologisk Tidsskrift*
EvTh	*Evangelische Theologie*
FRLANT	Forschungen zur Religion und Literatur des Alten und Neuen Testaments
GThT	*Gereformeerd Theologisch Tijdschrift*
HAT	Handbuch zum Alten Testament
HKAT	Göttinger Handkommentar zum Alten Testament
HZ	*Historische Zeitschrift*
IB	*The Interpreter's Bible*
ICC	The International Critical Commentary
IEJ	*Israel Exploration Journal*

JAOS	Journal of the American Oriental Society
JBL	Journal of Biblical Literature
JCS	Journal of Cuneiform Studies
JEOL	Jaarbericht van het Voorariatisch-Egyptisch Genootschap Ex Oriente Lux
JTS	Journal of Theological Studies
KAT	Kommentar zum Alten Testament
KBL	L. Koehler–W. Baumgartner, Lexicon in Veteris Testamenti Libros, Leiden 1953
KuD	Kerygma und Dogma
LXX	The Septuagint
MAOG	Mitteilungen der altorientalischen Gesellschaft
MT	The Massoretic text
MV(A)G	Mitteilungen der Vorderasiatisch(-Ägyptisch)en Gesellschaft
NJWJ	Neue Jahrbücher für Wissenschaft und Jugendbildung
NZSTh	Neue Zeitschrift für systematische Theologie und Religionsphilosophie
OLZ	Orientalistische Literaturzeitung
Or	Orientalia
OTS	Oudtestamentische Studiën
PAPhS	Proceedings of the American Philosophical Society
RA	Revue d'assyriologie et d'archéologie orientale
RGG³	Die Religion in Geschichte und Gegenwart, 3rd ed., Tübingen 1957–65
RHPR	Revue d'histoire et de philosophie religieuses
RSV	The Revised Standard Version
SBT	Studies in Biblical Theology
STK	Svensk teologisk kvartalskrift
StOr	Studia Orientalia
SupplVT	Supplements to Vetus Testamentum
TATT	Teologinen aikakauskirja. Teologisk tidskrift
ThB	Theologische Bücherei
ThLZ	Theologische Literaturzeitung
UH	Ugaritic Handbook
UUA	Uppsala universitets årsskrift
VAB	Vorderasiatische Bibliothek
VT	Vetus Testamentum
WC	Westminster Commentaries
WMANT	Wissenschaftliche Monographien zum Alten und Neuen Testament
WZKM	Wiener Zeitschrift für die Kunde des Morgenlandes
ZA	Zeitschrift für Assyriologie
ZAW	Zeitschrift für die alttestamentliche Wissenschaft
ZThK	Zeitschrift für Theologie und Kirche

Bibliography

The following list is not intended as an exhaustive bibliography of the subject of the present essay: it is simply a list of the works I have referred to or quoted. Well-known works of reference, such as grammars and dictionaries, have not been included.

Albrektson, B., 'Främreorientaliska och gammaltestamentliga föreställningar om uppenbarelse i historien. Några preliminära synpunkter', *TATT* 71, 1966, pp. 13 ff.
- *Studies in the Text and Theology of the Book of Lamentations. With a Critical Edition of the Peshitta Text* (Studia Theologica Lundensia 21), Lund 1963.
Albright, W. F., *From the Stone Age to Christianity. Monotheism and the Historical Process*, 2nd ed., Baltimore 1946.
- 'An Indirect Synchronism Between Egypt and Mesopotamia, cir. 1730 B.C.', *BASOR* 99, 1945, pp. 9 ff.
- 'Palestinian Inscriptions', *ANET²*, pp. 320 ff.
- 'A Third Revision of the Early Chronology of Western Asia', *BASOR* 88, 1942, pp. 28 ff.
Alt, A., 'Die Deutung der Weltgeschichte im Alten Testament', *ZThK* 56, 1959, pp. 129 ff.
Baillie, J., *The Idea of Revelation in Recent Thought*, New York 1956.
Balscheit, B., *Alter und Aufkommen des Monotheismus in der israelitischen Religion* (BZAW 69), Berlin 1938.
Barr, J., *Biblical Words for Time* (SBT 33), London 1962.
- *Old and New in Interpretation. A Study of the Two Testaments*, London 1966.
- 'Revelation Through History in the Old Testament and in Modern Theology', *Interpretation* 17, 1963, pp. 193 ff.
Barton, G. A., *The Royal Inscriptions of Sumer and Akkad* (Library of Ancient Semitic Inscriptions I), New Haven 1929.
Bechtel, G., see Sturtevant, E. H.
Bernhardt, K.-H., *Das Problem der altorientalischen Königsideologie im Alten Testament unter besonderer Berücksichtigung der Geschichte der Psalmenexegese dargestellt und kritisch gewürdigt* (SupplVT 8), Leiden 1961.
Böhl, F. M. T., *Der babylonische Fürstenspiegel* (MAOG 11: 3), Leipzig 1937.
Borger, R., *Babylonisch-assyrische Lesestücke*, I–III, Roma 1963.
- *Die Inschriften Asarhaddons Königs von Assyrien* (AfO Beiheft 9), Graz 1956.
Brandon, S. G. F., *History, Time and Deity. A Historical and Comparative Study of the Conception of Time in Religious Thought and Practice*, Manchester–New York 1965.
Bright, J., 'Hebrew Religion, History of', in *The Interpreter's Dictionary of the Bible* ..., 2, New York–Nashville 1962, pp. 560 ff.
Brundage, B. C., 'The Birth of Clio: A Résumé and Interpretation of Ancient Near

Eastern Historiography', *Teachers of History. Essays in Honor of Laurence Brad-
ford Packard*, ed. by H. Stuart Hughes, Ithaca, New York 1954, pp. 199 ff.

Budge, E. A. W., *Assyrian Sculptures in the British Museum. Reign of Ashur-nasirpal, 885–860 B. C.*, London 1914.

Budge, E. A. W.–King, L. W., *Annals of the Kings of Assyria. The Cuneiform
Texts with Translations, Transliterations, etc., from the Original Documents in
the British Museum*, I, London 1902.

Burrows, M., 'Ancient Israel', *The Idea of History in the Ancient Near East*, ed.
R. C. Dentan (AOS 38), New Haven 1955, pp. 99 ff.

Collingwood, R. G., *The Idea of History*, Oxford 1946.

Cullman, O., *Heil als Geschichte. Heilsgeschichtliche Existenz im Neuen Testament*,
Tübingen 1965.

David, M., *Les dieux et le Destin en Babylonie*, Paris 1949.

Delitzsch, Franz, *Neuer Commentar über die Genesis*, Leipzig 1887.

Delitzsch, Friedrich, *Assyrische Lesestücke* ... (Assyriologische Bibliothek 16), 4.
Aufl., Leipzig 1900.

Dentan, R. C. (ed.), *The Idea of History in the Ancient Near East* (AOS 38), New
Haven 1955.

Diakonoff, I. M., 'A Babylonian Political Pamphlet from about 700 B. C.', *Studies
in Honor of Benno Landsberger*, Chicago 1965, pp. 343 ff.

van Dijk, J., 'Une insurrection générale au pays de Larša avant l'avènement de
Nūradad', *JCS* 19, 1965, pp. 1 ff.

Donner, H.–Röllig, W., *Kanaanäische und aramäische Inschriften. Mit einem Beitrag
von O. Rössler*, I–III, Wiesbaden 1962–64.

Downing, F. G., *Has Christianity a Revelation?*, London 1964.

Driver, G. R.–Miles, J. C., *The Babylonian Laws*, I–II, Oxford 1952–55.

Driver, S. R., *The Book of Genesis with Introduction and Notes* (WC), 12th ed.,
London 1926.

– *A Critical and Exegetical Commentary on Deuteronomy* (ICC), 3rd ed., Edinburgh 1902.

– *Notes on the Hebrew Text and the Topography of the Books of Samuel* ..., 2nd
ed., Oxford 1913.

Duhm, B., *Das Buch Jesaja übersetzt und erklärt* (HKAT III: 1), 4. Aufl., Göttingen
1922.

Dürr, L., *Die Wertung des göttlichen Wortes im Alten Testament und im antiken
Orient. Zugleich ein Beitrag zur Vorgeschichte des neutestamentlichen Logosbegriffes* (MVAG 42: 1), Leipzig 1938.

Ebeling, E., *Bruchstücke eines politischen Propagandagedichtes aus einer assyrischen
Kanzlei* (MAOG 12: 2), Leipzig 1938.

Ebeling, E.–Meissner, B.–Weidner, E. F., *Die Inschriften der altassyrischen Könige*
(AOB 1), Leipzig 1926.

Eichrodt, W., *Theologie des Alten Testaments*, I–III, Leipzig 1933–39.

Eissfeldt, O., *Einleitung in das Alte Testament unter Einschluss der Apokryphen
und Pseudepigraphen sowie der apokryphen- und pseudepigraphenartigen Qumrān-
Schriften*, 3., neubearb. Aufl., Tübingen 1964.

– *Hexateuch-Synopse* ..., Leipzig 1922.

Eliade, M., *Le mythe de l'éternel retour. Archétypes et répétition*, Paris 1949.

Eppel, R., 'Les tables de la Loi et les tables célestes', *RHPR* 17, 1937, pp. 401 ff.

Falkenstein, A., 'Fluch über Akkade', *ZA* 57 (N. F. 23), 1965, pp. 43 ff.

Falkenstein, A.–von Soden, W., *Sumerische und akkadische Hymnen und Gebete*,
Zürich–Stuttgart 1953.

Fichtner, J., 'Jahves Plan in der Botschaft des Jesaja', *ZAW* 63 (N. F. 22), 1951 [printed 1952], pp. 16 ff.

Fichtner–Jeremias, C., *Der Schicksalsglaube bei den Babyloniern* (MVAG 27: 2), Leipzig 1922.

Finkelstein, J. J., 'Mesopotamian Historiography', *PAPhS* 107, 1963, pp. 461 ff.

– 'The So-called "Old Babylonian Kutha Legend"', *JCS* 11, 1957, pp. 83 ff.

Fohrer, G., 'Prophetie und Geschichte', *ThLZ* 89, 1964, cols. 481 ff.

Forrer, E. O., 'Eine Geschichte des Götterkönigtums aus dem Hatti-Reiche', *Mélanges Franz Cumont* (Annuaire de l'Institut de philologie et d'histoire orientales et slaves IV), 2, Bruxelles 1936, pp. 687 ff.

Fosbroke, H. E. W., 'The Book of Amos. Introduction and Exegesis', *IB* 6, New York–Nashville 1956, pp. 761 ff.

de Fraine, J., *L'aspect religieux de la royauté israélite. L'institution monarchique dans l'Ancien Testament et dans les textes mesopotamiens* (Analecta Biblica 3), Roma 1954.

Frankena, R., 'Het Epos van de Pestgod Irra', *JEOL* 15, 1957–58, pp. 160 ff.

– 'The Vassal-Treaties of Esarhaddon and the Dating of Deuteronomy', כה *1940–1965* (OTS 14), Leiden 1965, pp. 122 ff.

Frankfort, H., et al., *The Intellectual Adventure of Ancient Man. An Essay on Speculative Thought in the Ancient Near East,* Chicago 1946.

Freedman, D. N., 'The Chronicler's Purpose', *CBQ* 23, 1961, pp. 436 ff.

Friedrich, J., *Aus dem hethitischen Schrifttum. Übersetzungen von Keilschrifttexten aus dem Archiv von Boghazköi,* 1–2 (AO 24: 3; 25: 2), Leipzig 1925.

– *Staatsverträge des Ḫatti-Reiches in hethitischer Sprache,* 1–2 (MVAG 31: 1; 34: 1), Leipzig 1926–30.

Gadd, C. J., *Ideas of Divine Rule in the Ancient East* (The Schweich Lectures of the British Academy 1945), London 1948.

Gerleman, G., *Ruth. Das Hohelied* (BKAT 18), Neukirchen-Vluyn 1965.

Gese, H., 'Geschichtliches Denken im Alten Orient und im Alten Testament', *ZThK* 55, 1958, pp. 127 ff.

Goetze (Götze), A., *Die Annalen des Muršiliš* (MVAG 38), Leipzig 1933.

– *Ḫattušiliš. Der Bericht über seine Thronbesteigung nebst den Paralleltexten* (MVAG 29: 3), Leipzig 1925.

– 'Hittite Prayers', *ANET²*, pp. 393 ff.

– 'Hittite Rituals, Incantations, and Description of Festivals', *ANET²*, pp. 346 ff.

– 'Hittite Treaties', *ANET²*, pp. 201 ff.

– *Kleinasien* (Handbuch der Altertumswissenschaft, III. I. 3. 3. 1), 2. Aufl., München 1957.

– *Neue Bruchstücke zum grossen Text des Ḫattušiliš und den Paralleltexten* (MVAG 34: 2), Leipzig 1930.

– 'Die Pestgebete des Muršiliš', *Kleinasiatische Forschungen,* hrsg. von F. Sommer und H. Ehelolf, 1, Weimar 1930, pp. 161 ff.

Goossens, G., 'La philosophie de l'histoire dans l'Ancien Orient', *Sacra Pagina. Miscellanea biblica congressus internationalis catholici de re biblica,* ed. J. Coppens, A. Descamps, É. Massaux, I, Gembloux 1959, pp. 242 ff.

– '[Review of] Robert C. Dentan, The Idea of History in the Ancient Near East . . .', *BiOr* 13, 1956, pp. 187 ff.

Gordon, C. H., *Ugaritic Handbook. Revised Grammar, Paradigms, Texts in Transliteration, Comprehensive Glossary* (Analecta Orientalia 25), Roma 1947.

Gössmann, F., *Das Era-Epos,* Würzburg n.d. [1956].

Gottlieb, H., 'Den tærskende kvie – Mi 4, 11–13', *DTT* 26, 1963, pp. 167 ff.

Gray, G. B., *A Critical and Exegetical Commentary on the Book of Isaiah I–XXXIX* (ICC), I, Edinburgh 1912.

Gray, J., 'Social Aspects of Canaanite Religion', *Volume du Congrès, Genève 1965* (SupplVT 15), Leiden 1966, pp. 170 ff.

Grayson, A. K.–Lambert, W. G., 'Akkadian Prophecies', *JCS* 18, 1964, pp. 7 ff.

Grether, O., *Name und Wort Gottes im Alten Testament* (BZAW 64), Giessen 1934.

Gunkel, H., *Die Psalmen übersetzt und erklärt* (HKAT II: 2), 4. Aufl., Göttingen 1926.

Gurney, O. R., 'Hittite Kingship', *Myth, Ritual, and Kingship. Essays on the Theory and Practice of Kingship in the Ancient Near East and in Israel*, ed. S. H. Hooke, Oxford 1958, pp. 105 ff.

– 'Hittite Prayers of Mursili II', *AAA* 27, 1940, pp. 3 ff.

– *The Hittites* (Pelican Books A 259), rev. ed., Harmondsworth 1962.

– 'The Sultantepe Tablets (*Continued*). IV. The Cuthaean Legend of Naram-sin', *AS* 5, 1955, pp. 93 ff.

Güterbock, H. G., 'Die historische Tradition und ihre literarische Gestaltung bei Babyloniern und Hethitern bis 1200', *ZA* 42 (N. F. 8), 1934, pp. 1 ff.; 44 (N. F. 10), 1938, pp. 45 ff.

– 'The Vocative in Hittite', *JAOS* 65, 1945, pp. 248 ff.

Guthrie, H. H., Jr., *God and History in the Old Testament*, London 1961.

Gyllenberg, R., 'Kultus und Offenbarung', *Interpretationes ad Vetus Testamentum pertinentes Sigmundo Mowinckel septuagenario missae*, Oslo 1955, pp. 72 ff.

Hallo, W. W., *Early Mesopotamian Royal Titles: A Philologic and Historical Analysis* (AOS 43), New Haven 1957.

Harper, R. F., *Assyrian and Babylonian Letters*, Chicago 1892–1914.

Hehn, J., *Die biblische und die babylonische Gottesidee. Die israelitische Gottesauffassung im Lichte der altorientalischen Religionsgeschichte*, Leipzig 1913.

Hempel, J., *Altes Testament und Geschichte* (Studien des apologetischen Seminars 27), Gütersloh 1930.

– *Geschichten und Geschichte im Alten Testament bis zur persischen Zeit*, Gütersloh 1964.

Hendry, G. S., 'Reveal, Revelation', in *A Theological Word Book of the Bible*, ed. A. Richardson, London 1950, pp. 196 ff.

Hesse, F., 'Wolfhart Pannenberg und das Alte Testament', *NZSTh* 7, 1965, pp. 174 ff.

Hirsch, H., 'Die Inschriften der Könige von Agade', *AfO* 20, 1963, pp. 1 ff.

Hyatt, J. P., 'The Book of Jeremiah. Introduction and Exegesis', *IB* 5, New York–Nashville 1956, pp. 777 ff.

Jacob, E., *La tradition historique en Israël* (Études théologiques et religieuses), Montpellier 1946.

Jacobsen, T., 'Ancient Mesopotamian Religion: the Central Concerns', *PAPhS* 107, 1963, pp. 473 ff.

– 'Mesopotamia', in H. Frankfort et al., *The Intellectual Adventure of Ancient Man. An Essay on Speculative Thought in the Ancient Near East*, Chicago 1946, pp. 123 ff.

Jastrow, M., jr., *Die Religion Babyloniens und Assyriens*, I–II: 1–2, Giessen 1905–12.

Johnson, A. R., 'Hebrew Conceptions of Kingship', *Myth, Ritual, and Kingship. Essays on the Theory and Practice of Kingship in the Ancient Near East and in Israel*, ed. S. H. Hooke, Oxford 1958, pp. 204 ff.

– *Sacral Kingship in Ancient Israel*, Cardiff 1955.

Josefson, R., *Bibelns auktoritet*, Stockholm 1953.

Kammenhuber, A., 'Die hethitische Geschichtsschreibung', *Saeculum. Jahrbuch für Universalgeschichte* 9, 1958, pp. 136 ff.

King, L. W., *Babylonian Boundary-Stones and Memorial-Tablets in the British Museum*, London 1912.

- *Chronicles Concerning Early Babylonian Kings, Including Records of the Early History of the Kassites and the Country of the Sea*, I–II, London 1907.

- see also Budge, E. A. W.

Knudtzon, J. A., *Die El-Amarna-Tafeln* . . ., 1–2 (VAB 2: 1–2), Leipzig 1907–15.

Koch, K., 'Spätisraelitisches Geschichtsdenken am Beispiel des Buches Daniel', *HZ* 193, 1961, pp. 1 ff.

Köhler, L., *Theologie des Alten Testaments*, Tübingen 1936.

Kramer, S. N., *From the Tablets of Sumer. Twenty-five Firsts in Man's Recorded History*, Indian Hills, Colorado 1956.

- 'Sumerian Historiography', *IEJ* 3, 1953, pp. 217 ff.

- 'A Sumerian Lamentation', *ANET*², pp. 455 ff.

Kraus, H.-J., *Psalmen*, 1–2 (BKAT 15/1–2), Neukirchen 1960.

Labat, R., *Le caractère religieux de la royauté assyro-babylonienne* (Études d'assyriologie 2), Paris 1939.

Læssøe, J., *People of Ancient Assyria. Their Inscriptions and Correspondence.* Translated from the Danish by F. S. Leigh-Browne, London 1963.

Lambert, W. G., *Babylonian Wisdom Literature*, Oxford 1960.

- 'The Fifth Tablet of the Era Epic', *Iraq* 24, 1962, pp. 119 ff.

- '[Review of] F. Gössmann, Das Era-Epos . . .', *AfO* 18, 1957–58, pp. 395 ff.

- 'Three Unpublished Fragments of the Tukulti-Ninurta Epic', *AfO* 18, 1957–58, pp. 38 ff.

- see also Grayson, A. K.

Landsberger, B., 'Einige unerkannt gebliebene oder verkannte Nomina des Akkadischen', *WZKM* 57, 1961, pp. 1 ff.

Langdon, S.–Zehnpfund, R., *Die neubabylonischen Königsinschriften* (VAB 4), Leipzig 1912.

Laqueur, R., 'Formen geschichtlichen Denkens im alten Orient und Okzident', *NJWJ* 7, 1931, pp. 489 ff.

Lewy, J., *Forschungen zur alten Geschichte Vorderasiens* (MVAG 29: 2), Leipzig 1925.

Lindblom, J., 'Historieskrivningen i Israel och dess ställning inom forntidens hävdateckning', *STK* 11, 1935, pp. 211 ff.

- *Prophecy in Ancient Israel*, Oxford 1962.

- 'Die Vorstellung vom Sprechen Jahwes zu den Menschen im Alten Testament', *ZAW* 75 (N. F. 34), 1963, pp. 263 ff.

Luckenbill, D. D., *Ancient Records of Assyria and Babylonia*, I–II, Chicago 1926–27.

- *The Annals of Sennacherib* (The University of Chicago Oriental Institute Publications 2), Chicago 1924.

Malamat, A., 'Doctrines of Causality in Hittite and Biblical Historiography: a Parallel', *VT* 5, 1955, pp. 1 ff.

Mallowan, M. E. L., see Thompson, R. C.

Meek, T. J., 'The Code of Hammurabi', *ANET*², pp. 163 ff.

Meissner, B., *Babylonien und Assyrien*, I–II (Kulturgeschichtliche Bibliothek 1: 3–4), Heidelberg 1920–25.

- see also Ebeling, E.

Messerschmidt, L., *Die Inschrift der Stele Nabuna'id's, Königs von Babylon, enthal-*

tend die erste inschriftliche Nachricht über den Fall Ninives (MVG 1896: 1), Berlin 1896.

Miles, J. C., see Driver, G. R.

Moortgat, A., see Scharff, A.

Mowinckel, S., *He That Cometh*, Oxford 1956.

- 'Israelite Historiography', *ASTI* II, 1963, pp. 4 ff.

- 'Die vorderasiatischen Königs- und Fürsteninschriften. Eine stilistische Studie', *EYXAPIΣTHPION. Studien zur Religion und Literatur des Alten und Neuen Testaments Hermann Gunkel ... dargebracht ... (FRLANT N.F. 19), 1, Göttingen 1923, pp. 278 ff.

- 'Den västorientaliska och israelitisk-judiska litteraturen', *Bonniers allmänna litteraturhistoria*, ed. E. N. Tigerstedt, I, Stockholm 1959, pp. 13 ff.

Nineham, D. E., *The Study of Divinity. An Inaugural Lecture ... London 1960.*

North, C. R., *The Old Testament Interpretation of History*, London 1946.

- 'The religious Aspects of Hebrew Kingship', *ZAW* 50, 1932, pp. 8 ff.

- *The Second Isaiah. Introduction, Translation and Commentary to Chapters XL–LV*, Oxford 1964.

Noth, M., 'Geschichtsschreibung I. Im AT', *RGG³*, II, cols. 1498 ff.

- 'Das Geschichtsverständnis der alttestamentlichen Apokalyptik', *Arbeitsgemeinschaft für Forschung des Landes Nordrhein-Westfalen*, Geisteswissenschaften, H. 21, Köln und Opladen 1954 (=*Gesammelte Studien zum Alten Testament* (ThB 6), München 1957, pp. 248 ff.)

- 'Gott, König, Volk im Alten Testament. Eine methodologische Auseinandersetzung mit einer gegenwärtigen Forschungsrichtung', *ZThK* 47, 1950, pp. 157 ff. (=*Gesammelte Studien zum Alten Testament* (ThB 6), München 1957, pp. 188 ff.)

- 'Die Historisierung des Mythus im Alten Testament', *CuW* 4, 1928, pp. 255 ff.; 301 ff.

- *Überlieferungsgeschichte des Pentateuch*, Stuttgart 1948.

- *Überlieferungsgeschichtliche Studien. Die sammelnden und bearbeitenden Geschichtswerke im Alten Testament*, 2. Aufl., Tübingen 1957.

- *Das zweite Buch Mose. Exodus. Übersetzt und erklärt* (ATD 5), Göttingen 1959.

Nötscher, F., *Ellil in Sumer und Akkad*, Hannover 1927.

- 'Prophetie im Umkreis des Alten Israel', *BZ* N. F. 10, 1966, pp. 161 ff.

- 'Schicksalsglaube in Qumrân und Umwelt', *BZ* N. F. 3, 1959, pp. 205 ff.; N. F. 4, 1960, pp. 98 ff.

Nygren, A., *The Significance of the Bible for the Church* (Facet Books. Biblical Series 1), Philadelphia 1963.

- 'Uppenbarelsen och Skrifterna', in R. Bring et al., *En bok om bibeln*, 2. uppl., Lund 1948, pp. 85 ff.

Olmstead, A. T. E., *Assyrian Historiography. A Source Study.* (The University of Missouri Studies. Social Science Series III: 1), Columbia, Missouri, 1916.

Oppenheim, A. L., *Ancient Mesopotamia. Portrait of a Dead Civilization*, Chicago–London 1964.

- 'Babylonian and Assyrian Historical Texts', *ANET²*, pp. 265 ff.

- 'Zur keilschriftlichen Omenliteratur', *Or* N. S. 5, 1936, pp. 199 ff.

Östborn, G., *Yahweh's Words and Deeds. A Preliminary Study into the Old Testament Presentation of History* (UUÅ 1951: 7), Uppsala and Wiesbaden 1951.

Paffrath, T., *Zur Götterlehre in den altbabylonischen Königsinschriften* (Studien zur Geschichte und Kultur des Altertums 6: 5–6), Paderborn 1913.

Pannenberg, W. (ed.), *Offenbarung als Geschichte* (KuD Beiheft 1), Göttingen 1961, 3. Aufl. 1965.

Peiser, F. E., 'Die Monolith-Inschrift III Rawl. 7-8', *Keilinschriftliche Bibliothek*, ed. E. Schrader, I, Berlin 1889, pp. 150 ff.

Pering, B., 'Die geflügelte Scheibe in Assyrien. Eine religionsgeschichtliche Untersuchung', *AfO* 8, 1932-33, pp. 281 ff.

Pfeiffer, R. H., *State Letters of Assyria. A Transliteration and Translation of 355 Official Assyrian Letters dating from the Sargonid Period (722-625 B.C.)* (AOS 6), New Haven 1935.

Plöger, O., *Das Buch Daniel* (KAT XVIII), Gütersloh 1965.

– *Theokratie und Eschatologie* (WMANT 2), Neukirchen 1959.

Porter, J. R., 'Psalm XLV.7', *JTS* N. S. 12, 1961, pp. 51 ff.

Procksch, O., *Die Genesis übersetzt und erklärt* (KAT 1), 2. und 3. Aufl., Leipzig und Erlangen 1924.

von Rad, G., *Deuteronomiumstudien* (FRLANT N. F. 40), Göttingen 1947.

– *Das erste Buch Mose. Genesis Kapitel 1-12,9* (ATD 2), Göttingen 1949.

– *Gesammelte Studien zum Alten Testament* (ThB 8), München 1958.

– *Theologie des Alten Testaments*, 1-2, München 1957-60.

Ravn, O. E., 'Sumerisk og babylonsk-assyrisk religion', *Illustreret Religionshistorie*, ed. J. Pedersen, København 1948, pp. 131 ff.

Rendtorff, R., 'Geschichte und Wort im Alten Testament', *EvTh* 22, 1962, pp. 621 ff.

Ridderbos, N. H., 'Het Oude Testament en de geschiedenis', I–II, *GThT* 57, 1957, pp. 112 ff.; 58, 1958, pp. 1 ff.

Ringgren, H., *Israelitische Religion* (Die Religionen der Menschheit 26), Stuttgart 1963.

– *Word and Wisdom. Studies in the Hypostatization of Divine Qualities and Functions in the Ancient Near East*, Lund 1947.

Röllig, W., see Donner, H.

Rössler, D., *Gesetz und Geschichte. Untersuchungen zur Theologie der jüdischen Apokalyptik und der pharisäischen Orthodoxie* (WMANT 3), 2. Aufl., Neukirchen 1962.

Rudolph, W., *Chronikbücher* (HAT I: 21), Tübingen 1955.

– *Jeremia* (HAT I: 12), 2. Aufl., Tübingen 1958.

Scharff, A.–Moortgat, A., *Ägypten und Vorderasien im Altertum*, München 1950.

Schreiner, J., 'Segen für die Völker in der Verheissung an die Väter', *BZ* N. F. 6, 1962, pp. 1 ff.

Schroeder, O., 'Ueber *šaknu* in der assyrischen Königstitulatur', *OLZ* 20, 1917, cols. 174 ff.

Scott, R. B. Y., 'Isaiah Chapters 1-39. Introduction and Exegesis', *IB* 5, New York–Nashville 1956, pp. 151 ff.

Simpson, C. A., 'An Inquiry into the Biblical Theology of History', *JTS* N. S. 12, 1961, pp. 1 ff.

Sjöberg, A., *Der Mondgott Nanna-Suen in der sumerischen Überlieferung. I. Teil: Texte*, Stockholm 1960.

Skinner, J., *A Critical and Exegetical Commentary on Genesis* (ICC), Edinburgh 1910.

Smith, M., 'The Common Theology of the Ancient Near East', *JBL* 71, 1952, pp. 135 ff.

Smith, W. Robertson, *Lectures on the Religion of the Semites. The Fundamental Institutions*. Third Edition with an Introduction and Additional Notes by S. A. Cook, London 1927.

von Soden, W., 'Altbabylonische Dialektdichtungen. 1. Ein Hymnus an Nanâ für Samsuiluna von Babylon (1913–1875)' *ZA* 44 (N. F. 10), 1938, pp. 26 ff.
– see also Falkenstein, A.

Speiser, E. A., 'Ancient Mesopotamia', *The Idea of History in the Ancient Near East*, ed. R. C. Dentan (AOS 38), New Haven 1955, pp. 35 ff.
– 'The Biblical Idea of History in Its Common Near Eastern Setting', *IEJ* 7, 1957, pp. 201 ff.
– *Genesis. Introduction, Translation, and Notes* (AB 1), Garden City, N. Y., 1964.

Stephens, F. J., 'Sumero-Akkadian Hymns and Prayers' *ANET²*, pp. 383 ff.

Streck, M., *Assurbanipal und die letzten assyrischen Könige bis zum Untergange Niniveh's*, I–III (VAB 7: 1–3), Leipzig 1916.

Sturtevant, E. H.–Bechtel, G., *A Hittite Chrestomathy*, Philadelphia 1935.

Szeruda, J., *Das Wort Jahwes. Eine Untersuchung zur israelitisch-jüdischen Religionsgeschichte*, Łódź 1921.

Tallqvist, K., *Akkadische Götterepitheta. Mit einem Götterverzeichnis und einer Liste der prädikativen Elemente der sumerischen Götternamen* (StOr 7), Helsingforsiae 1938.
– *Der assyrische Gott* (StOr 4: 3), Helsingforsiae 1932.

Täubler, E., 'Die Anfänge der Geschichtschreibung', *Tyche. Historische Studien*, Leipzig–Berlin 1926, pp. 17 ff.

Thomas, D. W., *The Text of the Revised Psalter*, London 1963.

Thompson, R. C.–Mallowan, M. E. L., 'The British Museum Excavations at Nineveh, 1931–32', *AAA* 20, 1933, pp. 71 ff.

Thureau-Dangin, F., 'La fin de la domination gutienne', *RA* 9, 1912, pp. 111 ff.
– *Die sumerischen und akkadischen Königsinschriften* (VAB I: 1), Leipzig 1907.

Ullendorff, E., 'The Moabite Stone', *DOTT*, pp. 195 ff.

Ungnad, A., 'Der Gottesbrief als Form assyrischer Kriegsberichterstattung', *OLZ* 21, 1918, cols. 72 ff.

Volz, P., *Die Eschatologie der jüdischen Gemeinde im neutestamentlichen Zeitalter nach den Quellen der rabbinischen, apokalyptischen und apokryphen Literatur*, Tübingen 1934.
– *Der Prophet Jeremia übersetzt und erklärt* (KAT 10), Leipzig–Erlangen 1922.

Vriezen, Th. C., *An Outline of Old Testament Theology*, Oxford 1958.

Waterman, L., *Royal Correspondence of the Assyrian Empire*, Ann Arbor 1930–36.

Weidner, E. F., *Die Inschriften Tukulti-Ninurtas I. und seiner Nachfolger* (AfO Beiheft 12), Graz 1959.
– *Politische Dokumente aus Kleinasien. Die Staatsverträge in akkadischer Sprache aus dem Archiv von Boghazköi* (Boghazköi-Studien 8–9), Leipzig 1923.
– see also Ebeling, E.

Weiser, A., *Glaube und Geschichte im Alten Testament* (BWANT 4: 4), Stuttgart 1931 (=*Glaube und Geschichte im Alten Testament und andere ausgewählte Schriften*, Göttingen 1961, pp. 99 ff.)

Widengren, G., *The Akkadian and Hebrew Psalms of Lamentation as Religious Documents. A Comparative Study*, Stockholm 1937.
– 'Myth and History in Israelite-Jewish Thought', *Culture in History. Essays in Honor of Paul Radin*, ed. by S. Diamond, New York 1960, pp. 467 ff.

Wiseman, D. J., 'The Vassal-Treaties of Esarhaddon', *Iraq* 20, 1958, pp. 1 ff.

Winckler, H., *Altorientalische Forschungen*, 2: 1–3, Leipzig 1898–1901.
– *Altorientalische Geschichts-Auffassung* (Ex Oriente Lux II: 2), Leipzig 1906.

Wolff, H. W., 'Das Kerygma des Jahwisten', *EvTh* 24, 1964, pp. 73 ff. (=*Gesammelte Studien zum Alten Testament* (ThB 22), München 1964, pp. 345 ff.)

Wright, G. E., *God Who Acts. Biblical Theology as Recital* (SBT 8), London 1952.

— *The Old Testament Against Its Environment* (SBT 2), London 1950.

Würthwein, E., 'Gott. II. In Israel', *RGG*³, II, cols. 1705 ff.

Zimmerli, W., *Ezechiel* (BKAT 13), Neukirchen [1955 ff.]

— '„Offenbarung" im Alten Testament. Ein Gespräch mit R. Rendtorff', *EvTh* 22, 1962, pp. 15 ff.

van Zyl, A. H., *The Moabites* (Pretoria Oriental Series 3), Leiden 1960.

Indexes

A. MODERN AUTHORS

Thureau-Dangin, F., 18, 47, 56

Ullendorff, E., 100 f.
Ungnad, A., 44

Volz, P., 74, 89, 106
Vriezen, Th. C., 12

Waterman, L., 21
Weidner, E. F., 18 ff., 29, 41, 46 f.,
  50, 57, 63

Weiser, A., 14, 96
Widengren, G., 20, 96
Wilckens, U., 14
Winckler, H., 52, 59
Wiseman, D. J., 19
Wolff, H. W., 79
Wright, G. E., 11, 16, 118
Würthwein, E., 112

Zehnpfund, R., 36, 39, 43, 46, 93, 112
Zimmerli, W., 15, 86, 121
van Zyl, A. H., 100 f.

B. BIBLICAL REFERENCES

Gen.

12.1 ff.	78 f.
12.3	78, 80 f.
14.20	39 n.
18.18	80
22.18	80
26.4	80
27.28 f.	22
28.14	80
45.5	81
48.20	79 f.
50.20	82

Ex.

14.21	59 f.
23.31	39 n.
29.46	82
33.13	76

Num.

21.2	39 n.
21.34	39 n.

Deut.

1.27	39 n.
2.24	39 n.
2.30	39 n.
3.2	39 n.
7.6 ff.	118
7.24	39 n.
10.14 f.	118
11.2–7	113
20.13	39 n.
21.10	39 n.

28.1 ff.	22 n.
28.15 ff.	19
29.23 ff.	106
32.4	76

Jos.

2.24	38, 39 n.
6.2	39 n.
7.7	39 n.

Judg.

1.2	39 n.
1.4	39 n.
3.10	39 n.
3.28	39 n.
7.7	39 n.
7.9	39 n.
7.14	39 n.

1 Sam.

14.12	39 n.
28.6	117 n.

2 Sam.

7.10	83
7.13	83
7.14	51 n.
17.14	41
21.1	107 f.

1 Kings

9.8 f.	106
12.15	83
20.13	39 n.

Date Due

Demco 38-297